Winners' Guide to Essential ISEE/SSAT (Lower) Math -
(Grades 4-5)

Full coverage of all topics and sub-topics starting from the basics

By

A Anderson

Copyright Notice

CONTENTS

INTRODUCTION

Some students are naturally good at Math and tend to get overconfident or complacent.

On the other hand, there are students who shudder at the very thought of facing a math problem.

Well, neither of these approaches is conducive to a high math score.

What is required is a thorough study of the **fundamentals**, a basic grasp of the **concepts**, and developing an ability to **apply** these concepts to the SSAT/ISEE type problems.

Then comes the ability to solve a problem in **multiple** ways, the ability to use **shortcuts** when stumped, and the ability to **guess intelligently**.

Whether you are a natural at math or not, you *do* need to brush up /build up your fundamentals, and then go on to the more difficult problems under timed conditions.

And this is exactly what this book does.

It helps you to develop a **solid understanding** of the **underlying concepts**, builds upon this understanding by providing various **different types of examples** and finally allows you to practice your skills on the over 1000 problems.

Before you dive straight into the book, it is helpful to take stock of your current understanding of the Math concepts usually tested at the ISEE/SSAT Lower Level.

A **full length Math section test** is provided (with Answer Key at the end of the book) so that you can identify your strengths and weaknesses which should enable you to get the most from your study.

1. $50 + 28 =$

   _____

2. $110 - 24 =$

   _____

3. $8 \times 7 =$

   _____

4. Round 7852 to the nearest 100.

   _____

5. $18 + 21 \div 3 =$

   _____

6. Find the LCM of 12 and 42.

   _____

7. Reduce $\frac{20}{24}$ to its lowest form.

   _____

8. Change $4\frac{3}{7}$ into an improper fraction.

   _____

9. $\frac{3}{4} - \frac{1}{5} =$

   _____

10. $\frac{12}{5} \times \frac{2}{6} \div \frac{4}{3} =$

    _____

11. Arrange $\frac{3}{4}$, 0.9, 170% from the largest to the smallest.

    _____

12. Convert 9.12 into fraction.

    _____

13. Ray's salary for last year was $25,000. 15% of his salary is sales commission. How much sales commission did he get?

    _____

14. If a: b = 3: 4 and b: c = 2: 1, find a: b: c.

    _____

15. In a class, there are 6 boys and 14 girls. What is the ratio of the number of boys to the number of girls?

    _____

16. The ratio of the volume of lemon juice to the volume of water in a jug of lemonade is 1: 7. How much water is needed for 800 ml of lemonade?

_____

17. Given Δ*ABC is similar to* Δ*DEF*, find the unknown *x* in the figure.

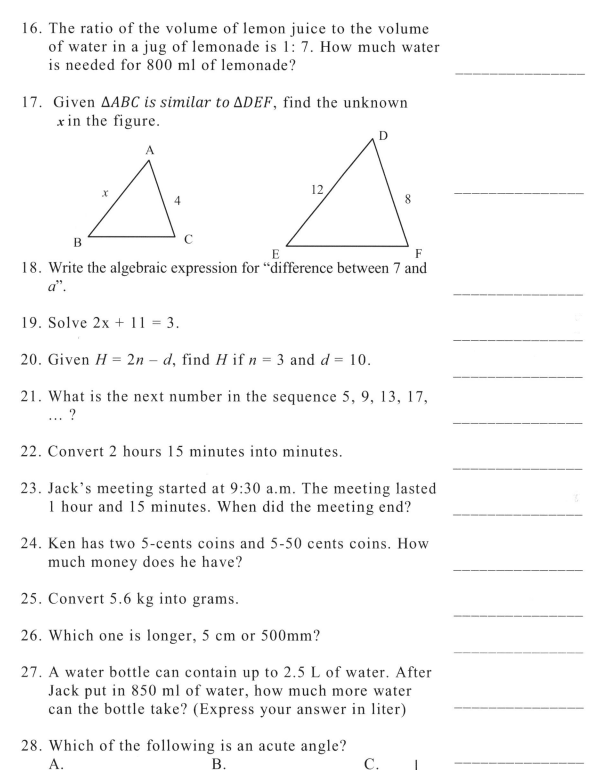

_____

18. Write the algebraic expression for "difference between 7 and *a*".

_____

19. Solve 2x + 11 = 3.

_____

20. Given $H = 2n - d$, find H if $n = 3$ and $d = 10$.

_____

21. What is the next number in the sequence 5, 9, 13, 17, ... ?

_____

22. Convert 2 hours 15 minutes into minutes.

_____

23. Jack's meeting started at 9:30 a.m. The meeting lasted 1 hour and 15 minutes. When did the meeting end?

_____

24. Ken has two 5-cents coins and 5-50 cents coins. How much money does he have?

_____

25. Convert 5.6 kg into grams.

_____

26. Which one is longer, 5 cm or 500mm?

_____

27. A water bottle can contain up to 2.5 L of water. After Jack put in 850 ml of water, how much more water can the bottle take? (Express your answer in liter)

_____

28. Which of the following is an acute angle?
A.   B.   C.

_____

29. What is the area of this triangle?

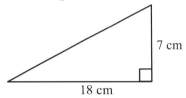

7 cm

18 cm

_____

30. There are four walls around a garden shed. Each wall is 6 meters long and 2 meters tall. A can of paint is enough to paint 8 m^2. How many cans of paint are needed to paint all four walls?

_____

31. Which of the following is a pentagon?

A.

B.

C.

_____

32. Which of the following is a pyramid?

A.

B.

C.

_____

33. What is the coordinate of point A?

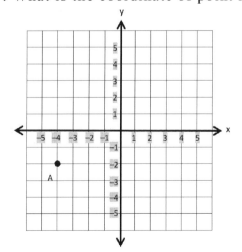

_____

34. Plot the image of the triangle after it is reflected against x-axis.

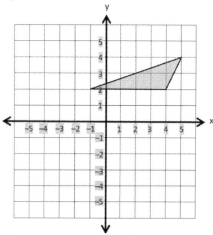

35. The coordinates of the vertices of a triangle are (-5, 2), (-4, 3) and (0, -2). If the triangle is translated 5 units right and 3 unit up, what are the coordinates of the vertices of its image?

_____

36. Complete the following symmetric figures with the given line of symmetry.

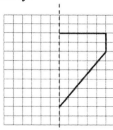

_____

37. How many books did Jack read in a week?

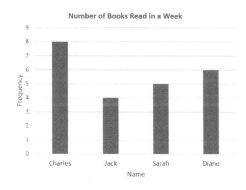

_____

38. On which day did the students borrow the most books from the class library?

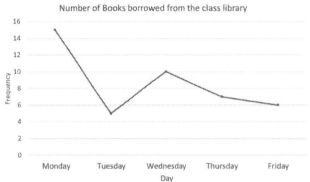

39. A survey result concerning sales tax is shown here.

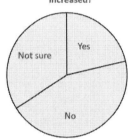

What do most people think about increasing sales tax?

40. According to the Venn Diagram shown below, how many students only join one club?

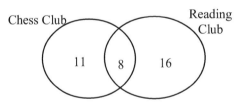

41. Find the mean of the following data set.
15, 19, 8, 6, 17, 20, 16, 11

_____

42. There are 14 cookies in a box. 5 of them are chocolate chips cookies. If a cookie is randomly picked from the box, what is the probability that it is a chocolate chips cookie?

_____

SYMBOLS

The first step in solving math questions is to understand the symbols that are used.

Here is a list of some of the common symbols you will encounter in your quest to master SSAT/ISEE mathematics.

Symbol	Denotes
$=$	Equal to
$+$	Plus
$-$	Minus
$\times$	Multiply
$\div$	Divide
$\neq$	Not equal to
$\leq$	Smaller than or equal to
$\geq$	Greater than or equal to
$<$	Smaller than
$>$	Greater than
$\%$	Percentage
$\sim$	Similarity
$\circ$	Degree of an Angle

Place Values

What is the difference between 328 and 823?
Is it necessary to write the zeros in the number 3006?

Section Objectives

- Understand what are place values and the importance of place values in the number system.
- Able to specify the place values of different digits in a whole number.
- Know how to write the number in expanded form, standard form and word form.

Key Study Points

Different digits in a number have a different values. For example, the number 3006 means three thousand and six. If the zeros in the middle are taken away, the number 36 represents a different value. 36 represents thirty-six where there are 3 tens and 6 ones.

Each place in a number has different values.

These values are called <u>place values</u>.

The following table shows the place values of whole numbers.

Ten millions	Millions	Hundred thousands	Ten thousands	Thousands	Hundreds	Tens	Units/ones	Value and word form of the number
				3	0	0	6	*3 thousands and 6 ones* Three thousand and six
						3	6	*3 tens and 6 ones* Thirty-six
2	0	4	3	0	5	1	1	*2 ten millions, 4 hundred thousands, 3 ten thousands, 5 hundreds, 1 tens, 1 ones* Twenty million four hundred thirty thousand five hundred eleven

Word form is using words instead of using numbers to represent the numbers (as shown in the rightmost column of the table above).

Expanded form is to write a number as a sum of the products of each digit and its place value. For example, the expanded form of 5692 is $5 \times 1000 + 6 \times 100 + 9 \times 10 + 2$.

Worked Examples

Example 1: What is the value of 9 in the number 239,000?

Ten millions	Millions	Hundred thousands	Ten thousands	Thousands	Hundreds	Tens	Units/ones
		2	3	9	0	0	0

The digit is at the thousands place. The value of 9 is 9000.

Example 2: Write 351,245 in word form.

When writing the word form, we can "cut down" the number by its commas.

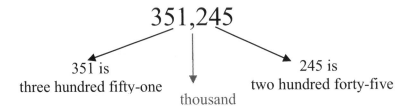

351 is
three hundred fifty-one

thousand

245 is
two hundred forty-five

We replace the comma with the word "thousand". Therefore, the word form of 351, 245 is three hundred fifty-one thousand two hundred forty-five.

(Note: In order to make large numbers easier to read, it is common to use commas every three decimal places in numbers of four or more digits, counting right to left.)

Example 3: Write 84,602,570 in word form.

First, we can "cut down" the number by its commas.

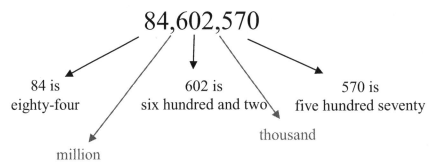

84 is
eighty-four

602 is
six hundred and two

570 is
five hundred seventy

thousand

million

We replace the comma on the right with the word "thousand" and the comma on the left with the word million. As a result, the word form of 84,602,570 is eighty-four million six hundred and two thousand five hundred seventy.

Example 4: Write seven million one hundred thousand nine hundred and four in standard form.

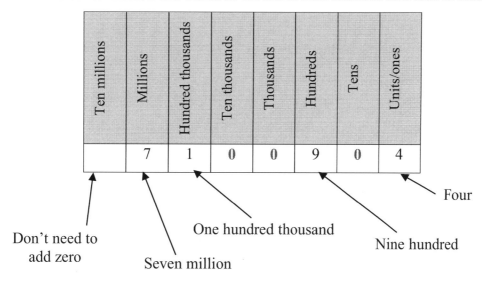

It is important to add the zeros between and to the right of the filled digits. (But not at the leftmost!)

After we added comma between hundreds and thousands places and between the million and the hundred thousands places, the standard form is 7,100,904.

Example 5: Write 78,073 in expanded form.

Ten millions	Millions	Hundred thousands	Ten thousands	Thousands	Hundreds	Tens	Units/ones
			7	8	0	7	3

After putting the digits in the number in the correct place, we can list out the expanded form according to the place value.

The expanded form of 78,273 is $7 \times 10000 + 8 \times 1000 + 0 \times 100 + 7 \times 10 + 3$

Practice Questions:

1. What is the value of 7 in the number 704,000?

2. What is the value of 2 in the number 5,027,678?

3. Write 978,535 in word form.

4. Write 1,241,080 in word form.

5. Write twenty-seven million, eight hundred thirty-three thousand, fifty-six in standard form.

6. Write one million, seven hundred four thousand, sixty-seven in standard form.

7. Write 50,247, 775 in expanded form.

8. Write 22,490 in expanded form.

Negative Numbers

 Are there any numbers smaller than 0?
Is negative 100 larger or smaller than negative 10?

Section Objectives

- Understand what negative and positive numbers are
- Able to use number line to locate positive and negative numbers
- Know how to compare positive and negative numbers

Key Study Points

All numbers that are smaller than zero are <u>negative numbers</u>. A minus sign in front a number shows that it is a negative number. For example, negative 3 is written as -3

Definitions

All counting numbers including '0' form the set of whole numbers.

Whole numbers are: {0, 1, 2, 3,......}

The whole numbers greater than '0' are called positive integers or natural numbers.

Natural numbers are; {1, 2, 3,......}

Corresponding to each natural number there is a 'negative' number that forms the set of negative integers.

Zero is neither positive nor negative.

Thus integers consist of negative integers and whole numbers.

Integers: {...., −3, −2, −1, 0, 1, 2, 3, ...}

The Concept of the Number Line; The number line is a straight line between negative infinity on the left to positive infinity to the right. (The symbol ∞ indicates infinity)

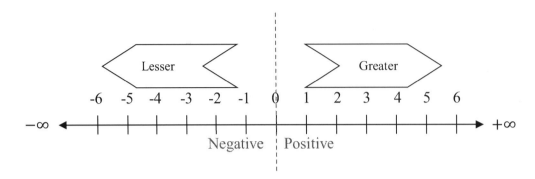

To compare numbers, there are a few rules to remember.

- The numbers on the left of the number lines are smaller than the numbers on the right
- Any positive number is larger than any negative number
- For negative numbers, the bigger the number the further away it is from zero

Worked Examples

Example 1: Find the values of a and b.

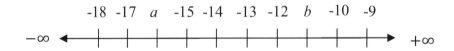

a is between -17 and -15 so the value of a is -16.

b is between -12 and -10 so the value of b is -11.

Example 2: Which of the following can be the value of *x*?

    A. -9

    B. -26

    C. -28

    D. -71

The smaller number is to the left on the number line. So, the value of *x* must be smaller than -28. Among the list of values given, only -71 is smaller than -28. The answer is D.

Example 3: Arrange the numbers from the least to the greatest.

$$-24, -63, 39, 71, -75$$

Remember, all the negative number should go to the beginning of the list because all negative numbers are smaller than a positive number.

Among the two positive numbers, 71 is greater than 39.

So, the list will end with 39 and 71.

Among -24, -63, -75   -75 is furthest away from zero as it is 75 units away from zero. -63 is closer to zero than -75. -24 is closest to zero. Therefore, -75 is the least and -24 is the greatest negative number in the list.

Combining positive and negative numbers, the answer is -75, -63, -24, 39, 71.

Practice Questions

1. Find the values of x and y.

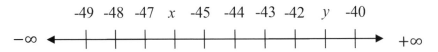

2. Find the values of p and q.

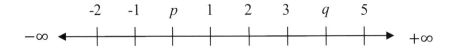

3. Which of the following can be the value of x?

   A. -3

   B. 9

   C. -8

   D. -4

4. Which of the following CANNOT be the value of y?

   A. -19

   B. 0

   C. 19

   D. -9

5. Arrange the numbers from the least to the greatest.

   -77, 16, -55, 66, 14, 0

6. Arrange the numbers from the least to the greatest.

   -85, -185, 85, -15, 15

7. Arrange the numbers from the greatest to the least.

   99, 39, -49, -69, 59, -29

Decimal Numbers

Are there any numbers between 1 and 2?
Is 1.06 smaller than 1.6?

Section Objectives

- Understand what decimal numbers are
- Able to use number lines to locate decimal numbers
- Know how to write decimal numbers in expanded form and word form
- Know how to compare positive and negative decimal numbers

Key Study Points

A <u>decimal number</u> is a number with a decimal point. The number of digits after the decimal points is called decimal places. For example, 33.4192 has four decimal places.

A decimal number can also be written in word form, expanded form and standard form like a whole number.

The digit to the immediate left of the decimal point represents the place of ones. The following table shows the place value for decimal numbers.

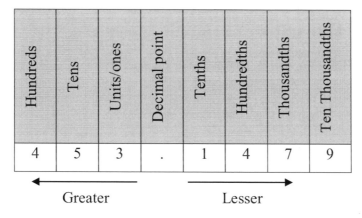

Hundreds	Tens	Units/ones	Decimal point	Tenths	Hundredths	Thousandths	Ten Thousandths
4	5	3	.	1	4	7	9

← Greater   Lesser →

The value of the place increases by 10 going towards the left. The value of the place decreases by 10 going towards the right.

The place value *tenth* means one part of the ten parts between each whole number.

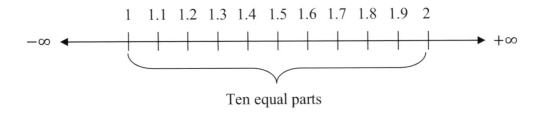

Ten equal parts

The number line below shows ten equal parts divided between 1 and 1.2

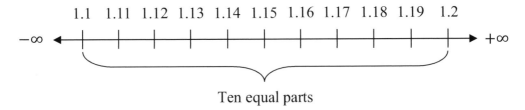

Ten equal parts

The above process of cutting down each interval into 10 equal parts can keep going for each decimal place down to the right.

When comparing decimal numbers, we can first compare the whole number portion of the decimal number. If the whole number portion is the same, make use of the place value table and compare place value starting from the tenths digit.

Worked Examples

Example 1: What does 3 represents in the number 2.372?

Hundreds	Tens	Units/ones	Decimal point	Tenths	Hundredths	Thousandths	Ten Thousandths
		2	.	3	7	2	

We can first fill in the digits from the number by using of the place value table. From the place value table, we can see that 3 is in the tenths place.

3 represents 3 tenths. *(Remember, do not mix up tenths with tens!)*

Example 2: Write 14.25 in word form.

Step 1: make use of the place value table to find out the place value of the digit.

Step 2: write the number to the left of the decimal point as we do normally with the whole number

Step 3: write "and" for the decimal point

Step 4: write the number to the right of the decimal point as we do normally with the whole number

Step 5: add the place value of the last digit

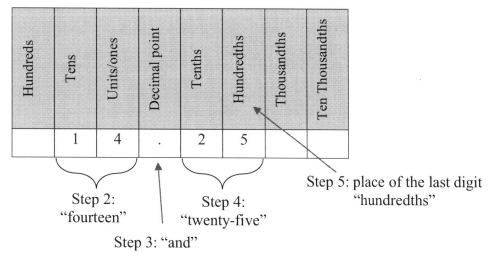

Step 2: "fourteen"

Step 3: "and"

Step 4: "twenty-five"

Step 5: place of the last digit "hundredths"

Therefore, 14.25 in word form is fourteen and twenty-five hundredths.

Example 3: Write 19.53 in expanded form.

Hundreds	Tens	Units/ones	Decimal point	Tenths	Hundredths	Thousandths	Ten Thousandths
	1	9	.	5	3		

With the place value table, we can find the place values of different digits.

$19.53 = 1 \times 10 + 9 \times 1 + 5 \times \frac{1}{10} + 3 \times \frac{1}{100}$

Example 4: Find the values of x and y.

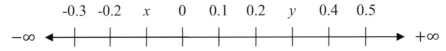

-0.3 -0.2 x 0 0.1 0.2 y 0.4 0.5

Each unit on the above number line represents 0.1.

x is to the left of zero so x is negative.

The value of x is -0.1 as we can count in steps of 0.1 from -0.2, -0.1, 0, 0.1, …

The value of y is 0.3 as we can count as 0, 0.1, 0.2, 0.3, 0.4, 0.5, …

Example 5: Arrange the list of number from the least to the greatest.

$$-2.93, -2.9, 1.7, 2.37, -1.73$$

First, we need to group the numbers into positive and negative numbers.

Positive: 1.7, 2.37

Negative: -2.93, -2.9, -1.73

For the positive number, we can quickly tell that 1.7 is smaller than 2.37.

For the negative number, -1.73 has the smaller whole number portion. However, since we are dealing with negative numbers, the smaller the number, the closer it is to zero. As a result, -1.73 is the greatest negative number in the list.

We can make use of the place value table to compare the other two negative numbers.

	Units/ones	Decimal point	Tenths	Hundredths
-	2	.	9	3
-	2	.	9	

If it is empty, pretend there is zero.

The comparison starts from tenths place. Since the tenths place is the same, we move down to hundredths place. For -2.9, the hundredths place is empty. So we can pretend there is a zero at its hundredths place. In this case, -2.93 is smaller than -2.9 as 2.93 units away from zero is further to the left of 2.9 units from zero.

So for the negative decimal numbers, the order from the least to the greatest is -2.93, -2.9, -1.73.

Combining positive and negative numbers, -2.93, -2.9, -1.73, 1.7, 2.37

Example 6: Which of the following cannot be the value of x?

A. 13.75

B. 17.17

C. -21.6

D. 17.77

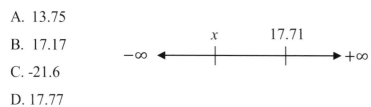

As x is to the left of 17.71, the value of x is smaller than 17.71.

-21.6 is a negative decimal number so it must be smaller than positive 17.71.

The whole number portion of 13.75 is smaller than the whole number portion of 17.71.

Tens	Units/ones	Decimal point	Tenths	Hundredths
1	7	.	7	1
1	7	.	1	7
1	7	.	7	7

The last step is to compare 17.17 and 17.77 with 17.71. We can do so by making use of the place value table. 17.17 is smaller than 17.71 as the tenths digit is smaller.

17.77 is larger than 17.71 as the hundredths digit is larger.

Therefore, the answer is D. 17.77 as it is the only value that is larger than 17.71.

Practice Questions

1. What does 8 represents in the number 2.832?

2. What does 4 represents in the number 351.014?

3. Write 34.7 in word form.

4. Write 127.074 in word form.

5. Write 2.9 in expanded form.

6. Write 7.456 in expanded form.

7. Find the values of x and y.

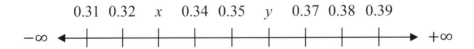

```
        0.31  0.32   x   0.34  0.35   y   0.37  0.38  0.39
-∞  ◄————┼─────┼─────┼─────┼─────┼─────┼─────┼─────┼─────┼————►  +∞
```

8. Find the values of m and n.

```
      -3.9 -3.89 -3.88   m  -3.86 -3.85 -3.84   n   -3.82
-∞  ◄————┼─────┼─────┼─────┼─────┼─────┼─────┼─────┼─────┼————►  +∞
```

9. Find the values of p and q.

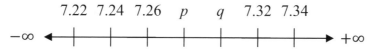

10. Find the values of a and b.

11. Arrange the list of number from the least to the greatest.

$$6.1, 6.15, 6.65, 6.6, 8.8, 8.76$$

12. Arrange the list of number from the greatest to the least.

$$3.2, 1.2, 9.22, 3.22, 1.22, 9.2$$

13. Arrange the list of number from the least to the greatest.

$$-4.25, 5.42, 4.25, -2.45, -5.42, 2.45$$

14. Arrange the list of number from the greatest to the least.

$$17.34, -17.345, -17.35, 17.3, -17.34, 17.35$$

15. Which of the following can be the value of x?

    A. 9

    B. 9.1

    C. 9.01

    D. 9.001

16. Which of the following cannot be the value of x?

    A. 6.6

    B. 6.06

    C. 6.666

    D. 6.65

17. Which of the following cannot be the value of x?

    A. -4.13

B. -10

C. -4.51

D. -9.15

18. Which of the following can be the value of *y*?

    A. 23.25

    B. 23

    C. 23.521

    D. 23.5

19. Which of the following cannot be the value of *y*?

    A. 11.6

    B. 7.89

    C. 7.99

    D. 9.79

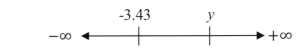

20. Which of the following cannot be the value of *y*?

    A. -3.34

    B. -3.44

    C. -3.3

    D. -3

Rounding Off

 Is there an easier way to write or read 4,301,029.43?

Section Objectives

- Understand what rounding off is
- Able to round off numbers by place values
- Able to round off numbers by decimal places

Key Study Points

Rounding off is a way to make it easier to deal with numbers yet be close to their exact value.

We use rounding off daily without thinking about it. For example, you would say there are about 800 students in your school whereas the actual number may be 822.

What makes us say 800 instead of 822? Intuitively, it is simpler to say 800 than 822.

Mathematically, 822 can be rounded off to 800 correct to the nearest hundred. As suggested by "correct to the nearest hundred", 800 is the nearest hundred number to 822. As on the number line shown below, 822 is closer to 800 than to 900.

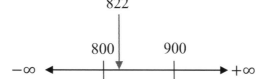

To decide whether to round up or down, we can imagine a line right in the middle of the two numbers. Any number that is 850 or above, can be rounded up to 900 as it is closer to 900 on the number line.

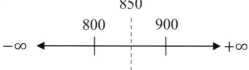

We do not have to draw a number line every time we are rounding numbers. When we are rounding 812 correct to the nearest hundred, we can draw line to the right of the hundreds digit. The line helps to remind us that the rounded number will have all zeros to the right of the line. Therefore, in this case, the rounded number will either be 800 or 900 as 812 is between 800 and 900.

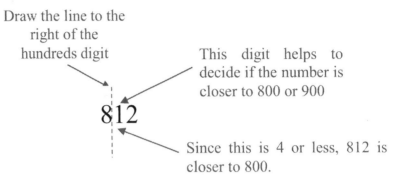

Draw the line to the right of the hundreds digit

This digit helps to decide if the number is closer to 800 or 900

Since this is 4 or less, 812 is closer to 800.

The digit to the right of the line helps to decide whether the number is closer to 800 or 900.

If the digit to the right of the line is 5 or more, the number is closer to 900

If the digit to the right of the line is 4 or less, the number is closer to 800

When we are talking about the number of students, it makes sense to think in terms of hundreds. However, when we are talking about the population of a city, we should think in terms of ten thousand. On the other hand, if we are rounding the weight of a chemical substance, it would make sense to think in terms of grams or even hundredth of a gram. In different situations, we are required to round off the numbers in different <u>accuracy</u>.

Here are some examples of different accuracy.

- Correct to the nearest hundred

- Correct to the nearest ten thousand

- Correct to the nearest tenth

- Correct to the nearest 2 decimal places

No matter what the required accuracy is, the steps to round the numbers are the same.

Worked Examples

Example 1: Round off 5.529 correct to 1 decimal place.

Since we need to round the number correct to 1 decimal place, we need to draw the line to the right of first decimal place. When 5.529 is correct to 1 decimal place, the rounded answer will either be 5.5 or 5.6.

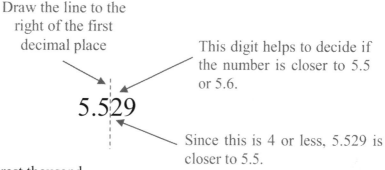

Draw the line to the right of the first decimal place

This digit helps to decide if the number is closer to 5.5 or 5.6.

Since this is 4 or less, 5.529 is closer to 5.5.

So, 5.529 = 5.5, correct to nearest thousand.

Example 2: Round off 11.35178 correct to the nearest hundredth.

Since we need to round the number correct to the nearest hundredth, we need to draw the line to the right of the hundredth place (remember do not mix up hundreds place and hundredth place). When 11.35178 correct to the nearest hundredth, the rounded answer will either be 11.35 or 11.36.

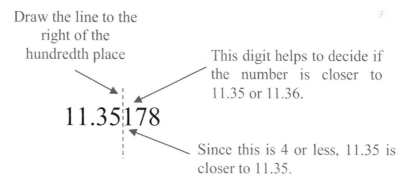

Draw the line to the right of the hundredth place

This digit helps to decide if the number is closer to 11.35 or 11.36.

Since this is 4 or less, 11.35 is closer to 11.35.

So, 11.35178 = 11.35, correct to the nearest hundredth.

Example 3: Which of the following cannot be rounded off from 36994.2?

    A. 36000

    B. 40000

    C. 36990

    D. 36994

We can try to correct the number to different accuracy and match the rounded numbers given. It is not necessary to try every accuracy. Based on the answers given, we should try

- correct to the nearest thousand for answer A (as the number in A has 3 trailing zeros)
- correct to the nearest ten thousand for answer B (as the number in B has 4 trailing zeros)
- correct to the nearest ten for answer C (as the number in C has 1 trailing zero)
- correct to the nearest one for answer D (as the number in D has no trailing zero)

When correct to nearest one, the rounded number will be 36994. Rounding to D is possible.

When correct to nearest ten, the rounded number will be 36990. Rounding to C is possible.

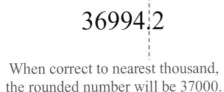

When correct to nearest thousand, the rounded number will be 37000. Rounding to A is not possible.

When correct to nearest ten thousand, the rounded number will be 40000. Rounding to B is possible.

After trying the possible accuracy, we can see that the number in answer A cannot be rounded from 36994.2.

Practice Questions

1. Round off 7114 correct to the nearest hundred.

2. Round off 347 correct to the nearest ten.

3. Round off 115706 correct to nearest thousand.

4. Round off 9756105 correct to the nearest ten thousand.

5. Round off 1.7506 correct to 1 decimal place.

6. Round 31.3245 correct to 2 decimal places.

7. Round 8.6226 correct to 3 decimal places.

8. Round off 3.0407 correct to the nearest tenth.

9. Round off 99.1186 correct to the nearest hundredth.

10. Round off 53.4996 correct to the nearest thousandth.

11. Round off 30999.9966 correct to

   a) the nearest ten thousand   e) the nearest one

   b) the nearest thousand   f) the nearest tenth

   c) the nearest hundred   g) the nearest hundredth

   d) the nearest ten   h) the nearest thousandth

12. Which of the following can be rounded off from 203050?

   A. 204000   C. 203100

   B. 203060   D. 210000

13. Which of the following can be rounded off from 62.97129?

   A. 62.98   C. 62.9712

   B. 62.971   D. 62.9

14. Which of the following can be rounded off from 45.69999?

   A. 46   C. 46.00

   B. 46.0   D. 46.000

15. Which of the following cannot be rounded off from 9273168?

   A. 9300000   C. 9273000

   B. 9270000   D. 9273160

16. Which of the following cannot be rounded off from 43.08465?

    A. 43.0847   C. 43.0

    B. 43.08   D. 40

17. Which of the following can be rounded off to 3600?

    A. 3510   C. 3670

    B. 3590   D. 3651

18. Which of the following can be rounded off to 7.0?

    (Correct to 1 decimal place)

    A. 7.0952   C. 6.9305

    B. 6.8912   D. 6.9731

19. Which of the following cannot be rounded off to 21600?

    A. 21602   C. 21581

    B. 21690   D. 21550

20. Which of the following cannot be rounded off to 4.00?

    (Correct to nearest hundredth)

    A. 3.9926   C. 3.9999

    B. 3.9953   D. 3.9969

Four Arithmetic Operations with Whole Numbers

What are sums, difference, product and quotient?

Section Objectives

- Review four arithmetic operations with positive numbers
- Able to determine which arithmetic operations to use in daily life situations
- Understand PEMDAS

Key Study Points

Addition is the process of combining two quantities. The numbers involved in addition are called addends. The result of addition is called sum. We add numbers in columns which can help us to align the numbers according to their place values.

Addition in columns

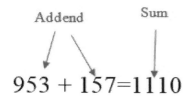

$$953 + 157 = 1110$$

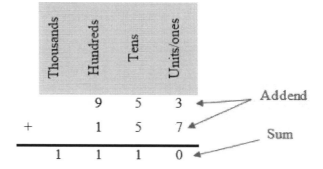

Remember to carry over when values exceed 10.

Addition is commutative, which means if we switch the order, we will get the same sum.

$$953 + 157 = 157 + 953$$

Subtraction is the process of finding difference between two quantities. The original quantity is called minuend and the quantity that is to be subtracted is called subtrahend. The result of subtraction is called difference. Similar to addition, we can do subtraction in columns to help us match up the digits according to its value.

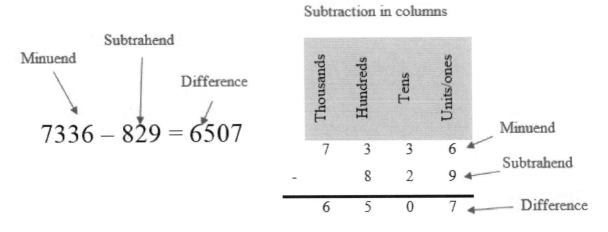

Subtraction in columns

$$7336 - 829 = 6507$$

Subtraction is not commutative. If we switch the order of the minuend and subtrahend, the difference will not be the same.

$$829 - 7336 \neq 7336 - 829$$

Multiplication is repeated addition. For example, 3×8 means 8 groups of 3. The number to be multiplied is called multiplicand. The number of times is multiplier. The result of a multiplication is product.

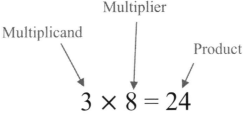

$$3 \times 8 = 24$$

For multiplication with smaller number, we can make use of repeated addition or a multiplication table. Multiplication is commutative. If we switch the multiplicand and multiplier, we will get the same product.

For bigger numbers, we make use of long multiplication. Like addition/subtraction in columns, we first align the numbers according to their place value. Then, we will multiply each digit in order shown below.

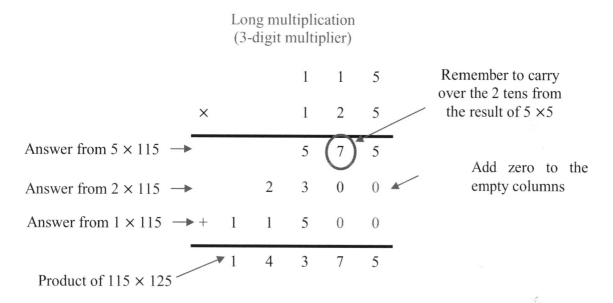

Remember to pay attention to carrying over when doing multiplication.

Division is the reverse of multiplication. It is used when we want to split up a quantity into groups of same size. 27÷3 means divide 27 into 3 equal groups. The number being divided is called <u>dividend</u>. The number of groups to divide into is call <u>divisor</u>. The result of a division is called <u>quotient</u>.

$$27 \div 3 = 9$$

Dividend · Divisor · Quotient

For smaller numbers, we can make use of the multiplication table to find the result. We can locate the dividend in the multiplication table and find the answers.

For example, if we want to find the answer of $42 \div 7$, we can locate 42 in the multiplication table and find that $6 \times 7 = 42$. As 7 groups of 6 makes 42, we can conclude that splitting 42 into 7 groups will give 6 in each group.

Sometimes, we cannot divide the quantity equally and there will be <u>remainder</u> with the quotient. For example, $45 \div 7$ will result in 6 groups but 3 remaining. Therefore, we can say **$45 \div 7 = 6R3$.**

For division involving bigger number, we will use <u>long division</u>.
Let us see how it works for 3929 divided by 12.

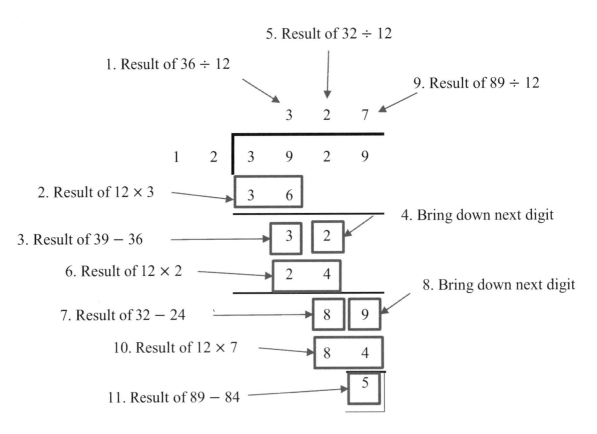

Therefore, $3929 \div 12 = 327$ R 5.

Divisibility Rules

1. A number is divisible by 2, when its last digit (unit's digit) is divisible by 2 or is 0, e.g. 266, 1760 and 442

2. A number is divisible by 3, when the sum of its digits is divisible by 3. e.g., 675, 160791

3. A number is divisible by 4 when the number formed by the last two digits is divisible by 4, or if the last two digits are 0 e.g., 7564 and 6600

4. A number is divisible by 5, when its last digit is 5 or 0. e.g., 245, 50

5. A number is divisible by 6, when it is divisible by 2 and 3 at the same time. e.g., 354

6. A number is divisible by 9, when the sum of its digits is divisible by 9. e.g., 432657, the sum being 27 which is divisible by 9

Arithmetic operations on even and odd numbers

1. even + even = even
   odd + odd = even
   odd + even = odd

2. even x even = even
   even x odd = even
   odd x odd = odd

3. even/even = even
   odd/odd = odd
   even/odd = even

The number 0 is an even number

PEMDAS

When there is more than one operation in an expression. We evaluate the expression in the order of **PEMDAS**:

1. P – Parenthesis
2. E – Exponents (We will discuss this in another section later)
3. M/D – Division or Multiplication
4. A/S – Addition/subtraction

Worked Examples

Example 1: Name the suitable arithmetic operations for the following situations.

(a) Janice opens a new box of printer paper and she is trying find out how many sheets of paper can she put into each of the four printers in the office.

Answer: Division as Janice needs to divide the box of paper among 4 printers.

(b) Ken buys a few bags of chocolate and there are 16 bars of chocolate in each bag. He wants to know how many chocolate bars there are in total.

Answer: Multiplication as each bag has 16 bars of chocolate.

(c) Sam measures his height every year and he wants to find out how much did he grow in last year.

Answer: Subtraction as Sam can get the growth from the difference in his heights in the two years.

Example 2: $48 \div 2 - (7 + 5 \times 2)$

Brackets should be evaluated first. But inside the brackets, the multiplication should be evaluated first. And outside of the brackets, division should be evaluated before subtraction.

$48 \div 2 - (7 + 5 \times 2)$

$= 24 - (7 + 10)$

$= 24 - 17$

$= 7$

Example 3: What is the smallest number that can be added to the number 7654981 to make it divisible by 4?

The last two digits of the given number are 81 which is not divisible by 4.

Since the number 80 is divisible by 4, we should add 3 to 81.

The resulting number will be 84, which is divisible by 4.

So, the answer is 3

Practice Questions

1. Name the suitable arithmetic operations for the following situations.

   (a) Josh built a tower with some blocks which are 5 cm tall each. Josh wants to find the height of the tower.

   (b) Beth has two ribbons of different length. She wants to find the total length of the ribbons she has.

   (c) A secretary works 48 hours in a week. Her boss wants to calculate her number of hours at work each day.

2. $1996 + 9365$

3. $296 + 1105$

4. $20464 + 1985$

5. $187 - 34$

6. $3206 - 797$

7. $47856 - 15761$

8. 6×35

9. 21×72

10. 957×13

11. $875 \div 5$

12. $231 \div 11$

13. $6064 \div 16$

14. $87 \div 4$

15. $368 \div 12$

16. $15788 \div 8$

17. $19 + 128 \div 8$

18. $48 - 3 \times 11$

19. $197 - 12 \times 15 \div 9$

20. $36 \div 4 + 12 \times 2$

21. $(79 - 15) \div 2$

22. $(187 + 65) \div 6 - 9$

23. $(2 \times 7 + 96) \div (11 - 6)$

24. $(22 - 72 \div 6) + 6 \times (17 - 3)$

25. $9 + (153 \div 9 - 5) \times 6 + (33 - 75 \div 5)$

Multiplying and Dividing by 10, 100 and 1000

 Is there a quicker way to do multiplication or division?

Section Objectives

- To know how to multiply by 10, 100 and 1000 quickly
- To know how to divide by 10, 100 and 1000 quickly

Key Study Points

Each place value is ten times more than the place value to its immediate right.

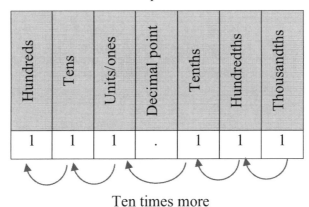

Ten times more

When we are multiplying a whole number by 10, we can quickly find the answer by moving the decimal points to the right once.

$$8 \times 10 = 80 \qquad 8. => 10 \text{ times} => 8\,0.$$

$$1.5 \times 10 = 15 \qquad 1.5 => 10 \text{ times} => 1\,5.$$

$$33 \times 10 = 330 \qquad 33. => 10 \text{ times} => 33\,0.$$

If the decimal point is already at the last place of the original number, remember to add a zero at the end of the number.

When we are multiplying a number by 100, we can quickly find the answer by moving the decimal points to the right twice.

When we are multiplying a number by 1000, we can quickly find the answer by moving the decimal points to the right 3 times.

$$0.72 \times 100 = 72 \qquad 0.72 => 100 \text{ times} => 0.72.$$

$$22 \times 1000 = 22000 \qquad 22 => 1000 \text{ times} => 22{,}000.$$

On the other hand, each place value is one-tenth of the place value to its immediate left.

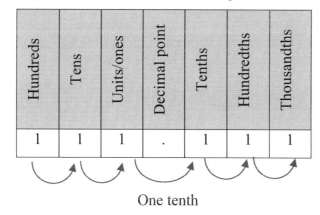

One tenth

When we are dividing a whole number by 10, we can quickly find the answer by moving the decimal points to the left once.

$$2 \div 10 = 0.2 \qquad 2 => \text{divide by } 10 => 0.2,$$

$$450 \div 10 = 45 \qquad 450 => \text{divide by } 10 => 45.0,$$

When we are dividing a whole number by 100, we can quickly find the answer by moving the decimal points to the left 2 times.

When we are dividing a whole number by 1000, we can quickly find the answer by moving the decimal points to the left 3 times.

$$36 \div 100 = 0.36 \qquad 36 \Rightarrow \text{divide by } 100 \Rightarrow 0.36.$$

$$4100 \div 1000 = 4.1 \qquad 4100 \Rightarrow \text{divide by } 1000 \Rightarrow 4.100,$$

Worked Examples

Example 1: 0.357×100.

$$0.357 \times 100 = 0.35.7 = 35.7$$

Remember to remove the zero at the front of the number if the decimal point is not at the front of the number.

Example 2: $150900 \div 1000$.

$$150900 \div 1000 = 150.900, = 150.9$$

Remember to remove zero at the back of the number if the decimal points are moved between non-zero digits.

Example 3: Is $849 \div 100 = 0.0849 \times 1000$ correct?

$$849 \div 100 = 8.49, = 8.49$$

$$0.0849 \times 1000 = 0.084.9 = 84.9$$

$849 \div 100 = 0.0849 \times 1000$ is Not correct.

Example 4: Is $0.135 \times 10 = 1.35 \div 100$ correct?

$$0.135 \times 10 = 0.1\,35 = 1.35$$

$$1.35 \div 100 = 0.01\,35 = 0.0135$$

No, $0.135 \times 10 = 1.35 \div 100$ is incorrect.

Practice Questions

1. 6×10
2. 28×10
3. 3.6×10
4. 0.09×10
5. 7×100
6. 41×100
7. 5.4×100
8. 6.99×100
9. 86.01×1000
10. 975×1000
11. 2350×1000
12. 19755×1000
13. $9 \div 10$
14. $700 \div 10$
15. $3.4 \div 10$
16. $64.3 \div 10$
17. $61 \div 100$
18. $20 \div 100$
19. $654 \div 100$
20. $5.4 \div 100$
21. $79 \div 1000$
22. $4387 \div 1000$
23. $3.5 \div 1000$
24. $0.986 \div 1000$

25. State if each of the following equations are correct or not.

    (a) $123 \times 10 = 1.23 \times 1000$
    (b) $9.61 \times 1000 = 0.961 \times 100$
    (c) $7.5 \div 100 = 0.75 \div 10$
    (d) $860 \div 1000 = 8.6 \div 10$
    (e) $44 \div 100 = 0.044 \times 100$
    (f) $2.95 \times 1000 = 29500 \div 10$

Four Arithmetic Operations with Decimals Numbers

 How do you find the answer to 35.3 – 1.97?

Section Objectives

- Review four arithmetic operations with decimal numbers.

Key Study Points

Like addition and subtraction for whole numbers, we also need to align decimal numbers according to the place values to find the right answers. For the empty columns, pretend there is a zero in that column.

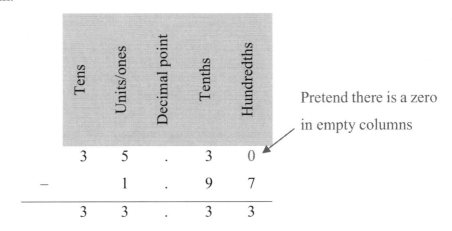

Tens	Units/ones	Decimal point	Tenths	Hundredths
3	5	.	3	0
–	1	.	9	7
3	3	.	3	3

Pretend there is a zero in empty columns

These are the steps for <u>multiplication of decimal numbers</u>.

Step 1: move the decimal points of the numbers to the right to change them to whole numbers.

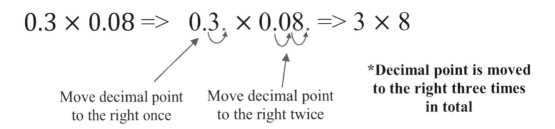

$$0.3 \times 0.08 \Rightarrow 0.3 \times 0.08 \Rightarrow 3 \times 8$$

Move decimal point to the right once

Move decimal point to the right twice

*Decimal point is moved to the right three times in total

Step 2: do the multiplication as usual.

$$3 \times 8 = 24$$

Step 3: move the decimal point of the answer to the left for the total number of times the decimal points of the multiplicand and multiplier were moved to the right.

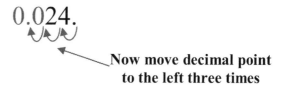

**Now move decimal point
to the left three times**

Therefore, $0.3 \times 0.08 = 0.024$.

The above steps are the same as multiplying 10, 100 or 1000 to the expression and then dividing the same number at the end to get the expression back to its original value. Here is an explanation of what is done in the previous 3 steps.

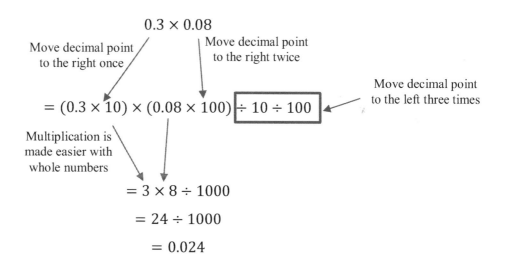

For <u>division of decimal numbers</u>, we also shift the decimal points of the numbers, but we are shifting them the same number of times. The goal is to make the divisor into a whole number.

$$0.9 \div 0.3 \Rightarrow \quad 0.9. \div 0.3. \Rightarrow 9 \div 3$$

Move the decimal points
to the right once

And then carry out the division as usual.

$$9 \div 3 = 3$$

So, $0.9 \div 0.3$ is the same as $9 \div 3$ which is equal to 3

If the decimal places in the dividend and divisor are different, we move the decimal places of the numbers until the divisor becomes a whole number.

$$0.924 \div 0.11 \Rightarrow \ 0.92.4 \div 0.11. \Rightarrow 92.4 \div 11$$

Move the decimal points
to the right twice

We stop after we move the decimal points to the right twice because then the divisor will become a whole number.

Then, we can ignore the decimal points in the dividend and do division as usual.

After we are done with the long division, we can put the decimal point back to the dividend. At the same time, we put the decimal point at the same place in the quotient

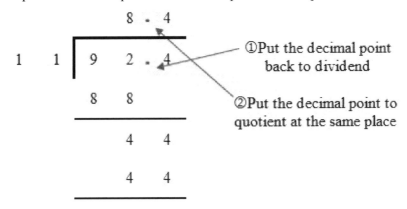

①Put the decimal point back to dividend

②Put the decimal point to quotient at the same place

The answer of $92.4 \div 11$ is the same as the original expression $0.924 \div 0.11$.

Therefore, the answer to $0.924 \div 0.11 = 8.4$

Worked Examples

Example 1: 58.1 − 27.954

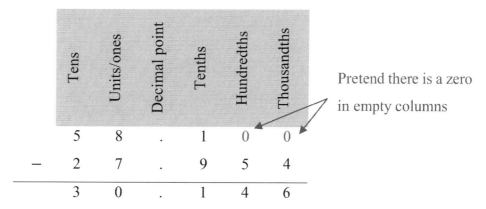

Tens	Units/ones	Decimal point	Tenths	Hundredths	Thousandths	
5	8	.	1	0	0	
− 2	7	.	9	5	4	
3	0	.	1	4	6	

Pretend there is a zero in empty columns

Example 2: 1.1 × 2.4

Step 1: move the decimal points of the numbers to the right to make them whole number.

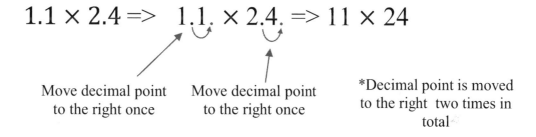

$1.1 \times 2.4 => 1.1. \times 2.4. => 11 \times 24$

Move decimal point to the right once

Move decimal point to the right once

*Decimal point is moved to the right two times in total

Step 2: do the multiplication as usual.

$$11 \times 24 = 264$$

Step 3: move the decimal point of the answer to the left for the total number of times the decimal points of the multiplicand and multiplier were moved to the right.

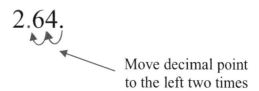

2.64.

Move decimal point to the left two times

Example 5: $1.88 \div 0.04$

First, we shift the decimal points for both the dividend and divisors the same number of times. Change the divisor into a whole number.

$$1.88 \div 0.04 \implies 1.88. \div 0.04. \implies 188 \div 4$$

Move the decimal points
to the right twice

Carry out the division as usual. Since $188 \div 4 = 47$, $1.88 \div 0.04 = 47$.

Example 6: $1.584 \div 0.8$

First, we shift the decimal points for both the dividend and divisors the same number of times. Change the divisor into a whole number.

$$1.584 \div 0.8 \implies 1.5.84 \div 0.8. \implies 15.84 \div 8$$

Move the decimal points to the right once

Then, we can ignore the decimal points in the dividend and do division as usual. Then add the decimal point back to the dividend and then put the decimal points in the same place for quotient.

```
              1 . 9   8
          ┌─────────────
        8 │ 1   5 . 8   4
              8
          ─────────────
              7   8
              7   2
          ─────────────
                  6   4
                  6   4
          ─────────────
```

Practice Questions

1. $21.9 + 43.7$
2. $3.197 + 45.6$
3. $19.05 + 113.7$
4. $4.61 + 0.678$
5. $98.6 - 45.7$
6. $515.7 - 123.29$
7. $64.5 - 2.38$
8. $115.78 - 81.5$
9. 7.5×0.2
10. 3.71×1.9
11. 6.4×2.74
12. 2.589×3.04
13. $7.2 \div 0.6$
14. $96.2 \div 1.3$
15. $5.52 \div 0.12$
16. $20.25 \div 2.5$
17. $10.36 \div 1.4$
18. $9.75 \div 0.075$
19. $75 \div 0.15$
20. $427.2 \div 0.24$

Four Arithmetic Operations with Negative Numbers

 What is the difference between $4 + 5$ and $4 + (-5)$?

Section Objectives

- Review four arithmetic operations with negative numbers.

Key Study Points

Adding a number means going forward (to the right) on the number line. Subtracting a number means going backward (to the left).

When both minuend and subtrahend are positive numbers, the difference will be a negative number if the subtrahend is larger than minuend.

$$3 - 5 = -2$$

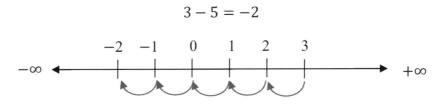

-5 means go backward 5 steps

When we are doing arithmetic operations with negative numbers, it is important to remember that **a number without a sign means it is positive.**

Adding a negative number is the same as subtracting a positive number.

$$3 + (-7) = 3 - 7 = -4$$

-7 means go backward 7 steps

Subtracting a negative number is the same as adding a positive number.

$$3 - (-7) = 3 + 7 = 10$$

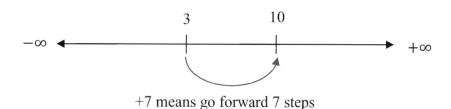

+7 means go forward 7 steps

And for multiplication and division with negative numbers, we need to remember these rules.

The product of TWO negative numbers is positive.

The quotient of TWO negative numbers is positive.

Worked Examples

Example 1: $9 - (-5)$

Recall that subtracting a negative number means adding the number.

$$9 - (-5) = 9 + 5 = 14$$

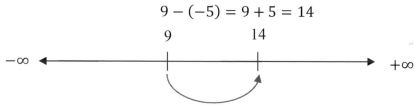

+5 means go forward 5 steps

Example 3: $-6 - (-11)$

Recall that subtracting a negative number means adding the number.

$$-6 - (-11) = -6 + 11 = 5$$

-6   5

$-\infty$ ←———————————————→ $+\infty$

+11 means go forward 11 steps

Example 4: $(-6) \times 7$

The product of one positive number and one negative number is negative.

$$(-6) \times 7 = -42$$

Example 5: $4 + 9 \times (-3)$

Recall the order of mixed operations. Multiplication/division is done before addition/subtraction.

$4 + \boxed{9 \times (-3)}$ ⟵——— Evaluate this first
Recall that the product of positive number and negative number is negative

$= 4 + (-27)$

$= 4 - 27$ ⟵——— Adding a negative number means subtracting that number

Example 6: $(-5) \times (-7) - 8 \div (-2)$

Pay attention to the sign – because it can mean subtract or negative. If the sign is between two numbers, the sign means minus because the sign of the operation goes between two numbers.

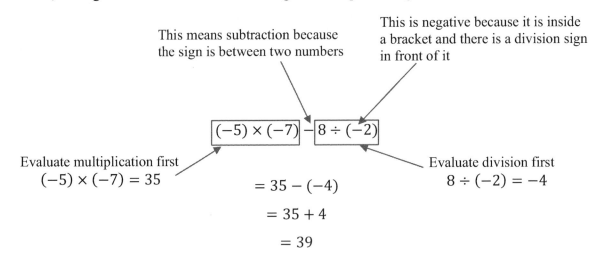

This means subtraction because the sign is between two numbers

This is negative because it is inside a bracket and there is a division sign in front of it

$\boxed{(-5) \times (-7)} - \boxed{8 \div (-2)}$

Evaluate multiplication first
$(-5) \times (-7) = 35$

Evaluate division first
$8 \div (-2) = -4$

$= 35 - (-4)$

$= 35 + 4$

$= 39$

Practice Questions

1. $3 + (-17)$
2. $-9 + (-9)$
3. $21 - (-9)$
4. $-4 - (-13)$
5. $-19 + (-7) + (-22)$
6. $31 + (-7) + (-16)$
7. $28 - (-32) + (-14)$
8. $-15 + 27 - (-12)$
9. $(-11) \times 7$
10. $(-5) \times (-31)$
11. $(-51) \div 3$
12. $36 \div (-4)$
13. $46 \div (-2) \times (-4)$
14. $27 + (-4) \div 2$
15. $(-88) \div 8 - (-14)$
16. $(-28) \times (-3) - (-8 + 7)$
17. $(-3.9) - (-1.7) \times 5$
18. $(-2.5) + 9.6 \times (-0.4)$
19. $(-3.68) \div 0.8 - (-1.4)$
20. $(-1.98 + 2.47) \times (-0.8 - 4)$
21. $(9.8 - 30.92) \div 0.8 \times (-2)$
22. $(-65.4) \div 1.09 - (-1.64) \times 0.25$

Factors, Multiples and Prime numbers

 Which number can divide another number without a remainder?

Section Objectives

- Understand what factors, multiples and prime numbers are
- Able to identify prime numbers and composite numbers
- Able to find the factors of composite numbers
- Able to list the multiples of a number and understand that the list of multiples does not end
- Able to determine if a number is the multiple or factor of another number

Key Study Points

Every number can be a product of two or more numbers. The numbers that we multiply together to get another number are called <u>factors</u>.

$$2 \times 5 = 10$$

2 and 5 are factors of 10.

Also, we can say that the number is <u>divisible</u> by its factors.

For example, 10 is divisible by 2 and 5.

<u>Prime number</u> is a number that has only itself and 1 as its factors.

It is a good idea to be aware of the first few prime numbers: 2, 3, 5, 7, 11, 13, 17…

2 is the only even prime number.

Numbers that are not prime numbers are called <u>composite numbers</u>.

All numbers can be written as the product of all its prime factors and this is called <u>Prime Factorization</u>.

Multiples are the opposite of factors. <u>Multiples</u> are what we get after multiplying a number with another number.

$$2 \times 5 = 10$$

10 is the multiple of 2 and 5.

To find the multiples, we can multiply the original number by 1, 2, 3, and so on.

Remember: The list of multiples can go on forever!

Worked Examples

Example 1: Find all the factors of 15.

$3 \times 5 = 15$

3 and 5 are factors for 15.

But, do not forget that $1 \times 15 = 15$. So, 1 and 15 are also factors of 15.

As a result, 1, 3, 5 and 15 are all the factors of 15.

Remember: 1 is the factor of all numbers. Also, the number itself is also its own factor!

Example 2: Find all the factors of 9. Is 9 a prime number or a composite number?

$1 \times 9 = 9$

$3 \times 3 = 9$

1, 3 and 9 are factors of 9. 9 is a composite number because 3 is also a factor of 9.

Example 3: Find the prime factorization of 24.

Divide 24 with smaller prime numbers until a prime number is left.

Keep dividing with prime number
$$24 \div 2 = 12$$
$$12 \div 2 = 6$$
$$6 \div 2 = \boxed{3}$$
Stop when only a prime number is left

Since we use 2 in the division process 3 times, remember to write it down 3 times in the prime factorization.

Therefore, the prime factorization of 24 is $2 \times 2 \times 2 \times 3$.

It is a good idea to check your answer by multiplying everything you write down for the prime factorization.

Example 4: Find the prime factorization of 180.

$$180 \div 2 = 90$$
$$90 \div 2 = 45$$
$$45 \div 3 = 15$$
$$15 \div 3 = 5$$

Remember, it is always good to try to divide the number by smaller prime number first. If the number is an even number, you can always start with dividing it by 2 until the result is no longer even.

Therefore, the prime factorization of 180 is $2 \times 2 \times 3 \times 3 \times 5$.

Example 5: Find the first 10 multiples of 5.

$1 \times 5 = 5$	$5 \times 5 = 25$
$2 \times 5 = 10$	$6 \times 5 = 30$
$3 \times 5 = 15$	$7 \times 5 = 35$
$4 \times 5 = 20$	$8 \times 5 = 40$

$9 \times 5 = 45$ $10 \times 5 = 50$

The first 10 multiples of 5 are 5, 10, 15, 20, 25, 30, 35, 40, 45 and 50.

Example 6: Determine if 6 is a factor of 76.

Since $76 \div 6 = 12R4$, 76 is not divisible by 6 so 6 is not a factor of 76.

Example 7: Determine if 84 is a multiple of 4.

Since $84 \div 4 = 21$, 84 is divisible by 4 so 84 is a multiple of 4.

Practice Questions

1. Find all the factors of 6.
2. Find all the factors of 25.
3. Find all the factors of 21.
4. Find all the factors of 18.
5. Find all the factors of 19.
6. Find all the factors of 29.
7. Find all the factors of 39.
8. Find all the factors of 100.
9. Find all the factors of 17. Is 17 a prime number or composite number?
10. Find all the factors of 27. Is 27 a prime number or composite number?
11. Find all the prime factors of 33.
12. Find all the prime factors of 42.
13. Find the prime factorization of 7.
14. Find the prime factorization of 30.
15. Find the prime factorization of 4.

16. Find the prime factorization of 44.

17. Find the prime factorization of 75.

18. Find the prime factorization of 8.

19. Find the prime factorization of 108.

20. Find the prime factorization of 675.

21. Find the first 5 multiples of 6.

22. Find the first 8 multiples of 4.

23. Find the first 6 multiples of 7.

24. Find all the multiples of 10 between 72 and 153.

25. Find all the multiples of 17 between 200 and 300.

26. State if these statements are true or false.

    (a) 6 is a factor of 3.

    (b) 39 is the multiples of 13.

    (c) 11 is the factor of both 55 and 121.

    (d) 38 is the multiple of 2 prime numbers.

    (e) A number can be a factor or the multiple of the same number.

    (f) A prime number does not have any factor.

    (g) A prime number can be expressed in prime factorization.

LCM and GCD

 What do 15 and 25 have in common?

Section Objectives

- Understand the concept of common factors and common multiples
- Able to find the highest common factor and lowest common multiple of two or more numbers

Key Study Points

GCD is the greatest common divisor that is common to two or more numbers.

GCD is sometimes also called **GCF** (Greatest Common Factor) or **GCD** (Highest Common Factor)

To find GCD of two numbers, we can list out all the factors and find the common factors. The highest of these common factors will be the GCD.

The factor of 24 are 1, 2, 3, 4, 6, 8, 12 and 24.

The factor of 54 are 1, 2, 3, 6, 9, 18, 27 and 54.

The common factors of 24 and 54 are 1, 2, 3 and 6. The GCD of 24 and 54 is 6

For bigger number, the following steps can be used to find the GCD more easily.

1. Write the numbers in their prime factorization
2. Find the common prime factors
3. The product of the prime factors will be the GCD of the numbers

For example, to find the GCD of 60, 84, 140.

Step 1: Writing the numbers in their prime factorization

$$60 = 2 \times 2 \times 3 \times 5$$

$$84 \ = 2 \times 2 \times 3 \times \quad 7$$
$$140 = 2 \times 2 \times \quad 5 \times 7$$

(It is a good idea to put the overlapping prime factors in the same column)

Step2: Find the common prime factors common to all the numbers

$$60 \ = \boxed{2} \times \boxed{2} \times 3 \times 5$$
$$84 \ = \boxed{2} \times \boxed{2} \times 3 \times \quad 7$$
$$140 = \boxed{2} \times \boxed{2} \times \quad 5 \times 7$$

Step 3: The product of the prime factors will be the GCD.

The GCD of 60, 84 and 140 is $= 2 \times 2 = 4$

Least common multiple (LCM) is defined as the lowest multiple which is divisible by all the given numbers.

To find LCM of two or more numbers, we can list out all the multiples until we can find the lowest common multiple.

The multiples of 4 are 4, 8, 12, 16, 20, 24…

The multiples of 6 are 6, 12, 18, 24…

The LCM of 4 and 6 is 12.

For bigger number, the following steps can be used to find the LCM more easily.

1. Write the numbers in their prime factorization by putting the overlapping prime factors in the same column

2. Write down the prime factor that appear in each column

3. The product of the prime factors will be the LCM of the numbers

For example, to find the LCF of 60, 84, 140

Step 1: Writing the numbers in their prime factorization by putting the overlapping prime factors in the same column

$$60 = 2 \times 2 \times 3 \times 5$$
$$84 = 2 \times 2 \times 3 \times \quad 7$$
$$140 = 2 \times 2 \times \quad 5 \times 7$$

Step2: write down the prime factor that appear in each column

$$LCM = 2 \times 2 \times 3 \times 5 \times 7$$

Step 3: The product of the prime factors will be the LCM of the numbers. So the LCM of 60, 84, 140 is $2 \times 2 \times 3 \times 5 \times 7 = 420$

Short cut method to find the GCD & LCM using factorization :

e.g., Find the GCD and LCM of 135, 270, 81

```
3 | 135, 270, 81
3 |  45,  90, 27
3 |  15,  30,  9
5 |   5,  10,  3
  |   1,   2,  3
```

The <u>common prime factors</u> of the 3 numbers are; 3,3,3

Therefore the GCD = 3 x 3 x 3 x 3 = 27

<u>All prime factors</u> of the 3 numbers are; 3, 3, 3, 5, 2, 3

Therefore, LCM = 3 × 3 × 3 × 5 × 2 × 3 = 810

Worked Examples

Example 1: Find the GCD and LCM of 15, 25 and 40.

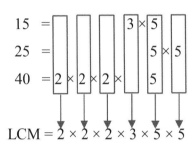

$$
\begin{aligned}
15 &= \quad\quad\quad 3 \times \boxed{5} \\
25 &= \quad\quad\quad \boxed{5} \times 5 \\
40 &= 2 \times 2 \times 2 \times \quad \boxed{5}
\end{aligned}
$$

GCD of 15, 25 and 40 is 5.

$$
\begin{aligned}
15 &= \quad\quad\quad\quad\quad \boxed{3} \times \boxed{5} \\
25 &= \quad\quad\quad\quad\quad\quad \boxed{5} \times \boxed{5} \\
40 &= \boxed{2} \times \boxed{2} \times \boxed{2} \times \quad \boxed{5}
\end{aligned}
$$

LCM = 2 × 2 × 2 × 3 × 5 × 5

LCM of 15, 25 and 40 is 600.

Example 2: Find the GCD of 2 and 7.

Since 2 and 7 are prime numbers, they only have 1 and themselves as their factor.

Factor of 2 is 1 and 2.

Factor of 7 is 1 and 7.

So, the factor of 2 and 7 is 1. GCD of any two (or more) prime numbers is 1.

Example 3: Find the GCD and LCM of 6 and 18.

6 is a factor of 18 and 6 is the largest factor of 6. The largest possible common factor can only be 6.

Factors of 6 are 1, 2, 3 and 6.

Factors of 18 are 1, 2, 3, 6, 9 and 18.

Therefore, GCD of 6 and 18 is 6.

18 is a multiple of 6 and 18 is the lowest factor of 18. The smallest possible common multiple can only be 18.

Multiples of 6 are 6, 12, *18*, …

Multiple of 18 are *18*, 36, …

Therefore, LCM of 6 and 18 is 18.

When we are looking for GCD of two numbers where one number is the factor of the other number, the smaller number is the GCD.

When we are looking for LCM of two numbers where one number is the multiple of the other number, the larger number is the LCM.

Practice Questions

Find the GCD and LCM of

1. 6 and 15
2. 12 and 18
3. 21 and 49
4. 24 and 40
5. 35 and 55
6. 8, 16 and 22
7. 20, 25 and 45
8. 24, 36 and 60
9. 45, 54 and 180
10. 125, 240 and 325

Square and Cube Numbers

What is the relationship between 2 and 8?

Section Objectives

- Understand what square and cube numbers are
- Able to find the squares and cubes of a number
- Able to say if a number is a square or cube of another number

Key Study Points

Square of a number means multiplying the number by itself.

The square of 4 is 16 because $4 \times 4 = 16$

We can also write it as $4^2 = 16$

Cube of a number means multiplying the number by itself *twice*.

The cube of 4 is 64 because $4 \times 4 \times 4 = 64$

We can also write it as $4^3 = 16$

The base shows us the number used in the multiplication. The Order shows us how many times to do the multiplication for.

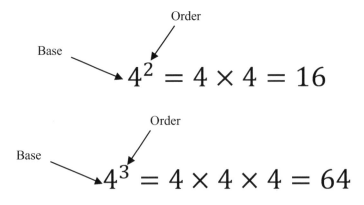

Remember the **square of a negative number is positive** because the product of two negative numbers is positive. So, all square number are positive.

$$(-5)^2 = 25$$

Similarly, **cube of a negative number is negative** because the product of one positive and one negative number is negative.

$$(-5)^3 = (-5) \times (-5) \times (-5) = 25 \times (-5) = -125$$

Worked Examples

Example 1: Find the square of 9.

$9 \times 9 = 81$

The square of 9 is 81.

Example 2: Find the cube of −3.

$$(-3)^3 = (-3) \times (-3) \times (-3) = -27$$

The cube of −3 is −27.

Example 3: Determine if 88 is a square number.

We can start to check if the given number is a square number by picking up a number whose square is close to the given number.

Since $9 \times 9 = 81$, we can start to check the square number of the numbers from 9.

But, $10 \times 10 = 100$.

So, 88 is not a square number.

Example 4: Determine if 396 is a cube number.

$7 \times 7 \times 7 = 343$

$8 \times 8 \times 8 = 512$

So, 396 is not a cube number.

Practice Questions

Find the square of

1. 8
2. 13

3. −6
4. −5

Find the cube of

5. 2
6. 11

7. −7
8. −8

Determine if the following numbers are square numbers.

9. 50
10. 100

11. −16
12. −388

Determine if the following numbers are cube numbers.

13. 29
14. 216

15. 278
16. −729

Fraction and Equivalent Fraction

 What is a number that lies between two whole numbers?

Section Objectives

- Understand the meaning of fractions
- Understand what equivalent fractions are
- Able to find the equivalent fractions
- Able to identify if two or more fractions are equivalent fractions

Key Study Points

Fraction is a part of a whole. The total number of parts is denominator and the number of parts is numerator.

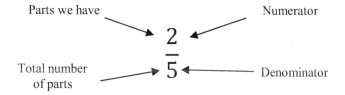

$\frac{2}{5}$ means two parts of a total of five.

The denominator of a fraction cannot be zero as division by zero is not defined.

Equivalent fractions are fractions with the same value. For example, $\frac{1}{2}$ has the same value as $\frac{2}{4}$. If we multiply or divide the **same number** to the numerator and denominator, we will get an equivalent fraction.

Fraction in the lowest term, also called the simplest form, means there is no common factors for the numerator and denominator.

To reduce a fraction, we divide the numerator and denominator with the Highest Common Factor of the numerator and denominator.

Worked Examples

Example 1: Reduce $\frac{4}{6}$ to the lowest term.

Remember, we divide the numerator and denominator with their GCD.

$$\frac{4}{6} = \frac{4 \div 2}{6 \div 2} = \frac{2}{3}$$

Example 2: Determine if $\frac{1}{10}$ and $\frac{2}{5}$ are equivalent fractions.

Since $\frac{1}{10}$ and $\frac{2}{5}$ are both in lowest term and they do not have the same numerator and denominator, hence $\frac{1}{10}$ and $\frac{2}{5}$ are not equivalent fractions.

Example 3: Determine if $\frac{15}{24}$ and $\frac{10}{16}$ are equivalent fractions.

First, reduce $\frac{15}{24}$ and $\frac{10}{16}$

$$\frac{15}{24} = \frac{15 \div 3}{24 \div 3} = \frac{5}{8}$$
$$\frac{10}{16} = \frac{10 \div 2}{16 \div 2} = \frac{5}{8}$$

Since the two fractions have the same value after they are reduced, the two fractions are equivalent.

Practice Questions

Reduce these fractions to the lowest term.

1. $\frac{4}{8}$

2. $\frac{5}{15}$

3. $\frac{9}{12}$

4. $\frac{10}{15}$

5. $\frac{12}{18}$

6. $\frac{36}{54}$

7. $\frac{81}{183}$

8. $\frac{16}{25}$

Determine if these fractions are equivalent fractions.

9. $\frac{3}{16}$ and $\frac{2}{8}$

10. $\frac{3}{15}$ and $\frac{1}{5}$

11. $\frac{6}{18}$ and $\frac{3}{9}$

12. $\frac{9}{21}$ and $\frac{3}{14}$

13. $\frac{4}{24}$ and $\frac{6}{10}$

14. $\frac{10}{28}$ and $\frac{15}{42}$

15. $\frac{4}{32}$ and $\frac{6}{48}$

16. $\frac{9}{42}$ and $\frac{6}{20}$

Mixed Numbers and Improper Fractions

 Is $\frac{9}{5}$ a fraction?

Can a fraction be bigger than 1?

Section Objectives

- Understand what are proper fractions, improper fractions and mixed numbers

Key Study Points

A fraction whose numerator is less than its denominator is called a **proper fraction.**

For example, $\frac{3}{5}$ is a proper fraction.

A fraction whose numerator is equal to or greater than its denominator is called **improper fraction.**

For example, $\frac{5}{3}$ is an improper fraction.

A fraction that consists of two parts, a whole number and a fraction is called a **mixed number.**

(**Note:** A mixed number can always be written as an improper fraction and an improper fraction can always be written as a mixed number.)

For example, $5\frac{3}{5}$ is a mixed number. '5' is the whole number and $\frac{3}{5}$ is the fractional part.

To change a <u>mixed number to a fraction</u>, we should keep the original denominator and find the new numerator by multiplying the whole number with the denominator and add the original numerator.

For example, $4\frac{3}{5} = 4 + \frac{3}{5} = \frac{4 \times 5 + 3}{5} = \frac{23}{5}$

To change an improper fraction to a mixed number, we should divide the original numerator with the original denominator.

For example, $23 \div 5 = 4R3$.

$$\frac{23}{5} = 4\frac{3}{5}$$

Practice Questions

Determine if each of the following is a proper fraction, improper fraction or mixed number.

1. $\frac{9}{4}$

2. $3\frac{5}{7}$

3. $\frac{11}{5}$

4. $\frac{4}{8}$

5. $\frac{9}{19}$

6. $11\frac{1}{2}$

Change the following into improper fractions.

7. $2\frac{2}{5}$

8. $1\frac{7}{9}$

9. $3\frac{4}{5}$

10. $7\frac{6}{7}$

11. $3\frac{1}{4}$

12. $5\frac{3}{7}$

Change the following into mixed numbers.

13. $\frac{4}{3}$

14. $\frac{14}{5}$

15. $\frac{19}{7}$

16. $\frac{34}{11}$

17. $\frac{53}{12}$

18. $\frac{91}{24}$

Multiplying and Dividing Fractions

 How can you find a quarter of two-thirds?

Section Objectives

- Able to evaluate the multiplication or division of fractions and mixed numbers

Key Study Points

To multiply and divide fractions, remember to do the following:

- Change all mixed numbers into improper fractions.
- Multiply denominators to denominators and multiply numerators to numerators.
- In case of division, switch the denominator and numerator of divisor.
- Remember to simplify the answers.

Worked Examples

Example 1: $\frac{9}{10} \times 2\frac{1}{2}$

$$\frac{9}{10} \times 2\frac{1}{2} = \frac{9}{10} \times \frac{5}{2} \qquad \text{change all mixed numbers into fractions}$$

$$= \frac{9 \times 5}{10 \times 2} \qquad \text{Multiply denominators to denominators}$$

$$\text{Multiply numerators to numerators}$$

$$= \frac{45}{20}$$

$$= \frac{9}{4} \qquad \text{Simplify the answer}$$

Example 2: $2\frac{1}{7} \div \frac{25}{14}$

$$2\frac{1}{7} \div \frac{25}{14} = \frac{15}{7} \div \frac{25}{14}$$

change all mixed numbers into fractions

$$= \frac{15}{7} \times \frac{14}{25}$$

Switch the denominator and numerator of divisor

$$= \frac{3\cancel{15}}{1\cancel{7}} \times \frac{\cancel{14}\,2}{\cancel{25}\,5} = \frac{3}{1} \times \frac{2}{5}$$

Simply the fractions before multiplying

$$= \frac{6}{5}$$

Multiply denominators to denominators

Multiply numerators to numerators

Example 3: In the fridge, there was $\frac{7}{8}$ of pizza. Sam ate half of the pizza in the fridge. What fraction of the whole pizza did Sam eat?

To find half of $\frac{7}{8}$, we need to use multiplication.

$$\frac{7}{8} \times \frac{1}{2} = \frac{7 \times 1}{8 \times 2} = \frac{7}{16}$$

Sam ate $\frac{7}{16}$ of the pizza.

Example 4: A team of construction workers finishes building $\frac{3}{10}$ km of a bridge in a week. If the finished bridge should be $2\frac{2}{5}$ km long, how long should the building of the bridge take?

We should use division to find the number of weeks needed to build the bridge.

$$2\frac{2}{5} \div \frac{3}{10} = \frac{12}{5} \div \frac{3}{10} = \frac{12}{5} \times \frac{10}{3} = 8$$

The bridge should take 8 weeks to build.

Practice Questions

1. $\frac{1}{5} \times \frac{8}{3}$

2. $\frac{2}{7} \times \frac{8}{3}$

3. $\frac{9}{4} \times \frac{4}{5}$

4. $\frac{27}{20} \times \frac{5}{6}$

5. $\frac{5}{7} \div \frac{3}{4}$

6. $\frac{8}{5} \div \frac{7}{2}$

7. $\frac{5}{22} \div \frac{5}{9}$

8. $\frac{18}{25} \div \frac{21}{10}$

9. $1\frac{3}{5} \times \frac{3}{7}$

10. $\frac{8}{9} \times 2\frac{2}{9}$

11. $3\frac{1}{2} \times 1\frac{1}{3}$

12. $4\frac{2}{3} \times 2\frac{1}{7}$

13. $1\frac{2}{7} \div \frac{3}{4}$

14. $\frac{4}{27} \div 2\frac{2}{9}$

15. $6\frac{1}{4} \div 2\frac{1}{7}$

16. $2\frac{2}{5} \div 6\frac{2}{3}$

17. $\frac{9}{10} \times \frac{5}{7} \div \frac{15}{14}$

18. $\frac{32}{25} \div \frac{10}{3} \times \frac{5}{8}$

19. $1\frac{3}{5} \times \frac{7}{8} \div 4\frac{2}{3}$

20. $1\frac{7}{21} \div 3\frac{3}{5} \times \frac{7}{30}$

21. Henry reads $\frac{3}{8}$ of a book every day. How much can he read in 6 days?

22. Nancy earned $\$7\frac{3}{4}$ every hour. If she worked $5\frac{1}{3}$ hours on Wednesday, how much did she earn on Wednesday?

23. Fred had $\$15\frac{1}{2}$ allowance for 5 days. How much money can he spend each day?

24. Ben ran $1\frac{1}{4}$ km a day. In March, Ben ran the total distance of $27\frac{1}{2}$ km. How many days did he run in March?

25. In a tailor shop, 5 tailors can make $9\frac{3}{8}$ jackets in $2\frac{1}{2}$ hours. How many jackets can one tailor make in $3\frac{1}{3}$ hours?

Comparing Fractions

 Is $\frac{1}{8}$ larger than $\frac{1}{6}$?

Section Objectives

- Able to find the common denominator of two or more fractions
- Know how to compare fractions with like or unlike denominator

Key Study Points

When two fractions have <u>like denominator</u>, the fraction with larger numerator is larger.

For example, $\frac{1}{4} < \frac{3}{4}$

When two fractions have <u>unlike denominator</u>, we need to change the fractions into fractions with a common denominator and compare the numerator. The LCM of the denominators is the common denominator. Then, we need to expand the fractions and compare the numerators.

For example, when comparing $\frac{5}{12}$ and $\frac{3}{8}$,

Step 1: find the LCM of 12 and 8

LCM of 12 and 8 is 24.

Step 2: expand the fractions.

$$\frac{5}{12} = \frac{5 \times 2}{12 \times 2} = \frac{10}{24}$$
$$\frac{3}{8} = \frac{3 \times 3}{8 \times 3} = \frac{9}{24}$$

Step 3: compare the numerators.

Since $\frac{10}{24} > \frac{9}{24}$, $\frac{5}{12}$ is larger than $\frac{3}{8}$

When two fractions have the <u>same numerator</u>, the fraction that has a larger denominator is smaller.

For example, $\frac{1}{4} < \frac{1}{2}$

Worked Examples

Example 1: Find the largest fraction among $\frac{1}{6}, \frac{3}{20}$ and $\frac{2}{5}$.

Step 1: find the LCM of 6, 20 and 5.

The LCM of 6, 20 and 5 is 60

Step 2: expand the fractions.

$$\frac{1}{6} = \frac{1 \times 10}{6 \times 10} = \frac{10}{60}$$

$$\frac{3}{20} = \frac{3 \times 3}{20 \times 3} = \frac{9}{60}$$

$$\frac{2}{5} = \frac{2 \times 12}{5 \times 12} = \frac{24}{60}$$

Step 3: compare the numerators.

$\frac{24}{60}$ is the largest among the three new fractions. Therefore, $\frac{2}{5}$ is the largest fraction.

Practice Questions

Arrange these fractions from the least to the largest.

1. $\dfrac{1}{7}, \dfrac{3}{7}$

2. $\dfrac{2}{5}, \dfrac{2}{3}$

3. $\dfrac{7}{12}, \dfrac{5}{9}$

4. $\dfrac{5}{7}, \dfrac{5}{9}, \dfrac{5}{6}$

5. $\dfrac{2}{3}, \dfrac{7}{15}, \dfrac{5}{12}$

6. $\dfrac{13}{16}, \dfrac{11}{24}, \dfrac{7}{18}$

7. $1\dfrac{1}{7}, \dfrac{9}{7}, \dfrac{3}{7}$

8. $\dfrac{11}{6}, 1\dfrac{1}{4}, \dfrac{11}{10}$

9. $1\dfrac{17}{24}, 2\dfrac{1}{16}, \dfrac{41}{32}$

Arrange these fractions from the largest to the least.

10. $\dfrac{1}{8}, \dfrac{7}{8}$

11. $\dfrac{2}{4}, \dfrac{2}{7}$

12. $\dfrac{5}{18}, \dfrac{8}{15}$

13. $\dfrac{3}{11}, \dfrac{3}{8}, \dfrac{3}{14}$

14. $\dfrac{5}{6}, \dfrac{4}{9}, \dfrac{11}{15}$

15. $\dfrac{10}{21}, \dfrac{11}{49}, \dfrac{5}{27}$

16. $\dfrac{8}{5}, 1\dfrac{4}{5}, \dfrac{3}{5}$

17. $\dfrac{7}{3}, \dfrac{22}{15}, 2\dfrac{5}{12}$

18. $2\dfrac{17}{25}, \dfrac{63}{20}, 3\dfrac{1}{15}$

19. The ceiling in Joan's house is $2\dfrac{9}{10}$ meters tall. Joan wants to buy a Christmas tree that is $\dfrac{21}{5}$ meters tall. Can the Christmas tree fit in her house?

20. There are two bus routes to go from Jacky's house to the school. The first route takes $\dfrac{7}{12}$ hour and the second route takes $\dfrac{2}{3}$ hour. Which route is faster?

21. In a week, Alfred ran $\dfrac{22}{3}$ km and biked $7\dfrac{2}{3}$ km. Did he run more or bike more?

22. Claire needs $\dfrac{7}{10}$ meters of ribbons for her art project and she finds $\dfrac{5}{9}$ meter of ribbons at home. Does she have enough ribbons for her project?

Adding and Subtracting fractions

 How to find the total of $\frac{1}{3}$ and $\frac{2}{5}$?

Section Objectives

- Able to perform addition or subtraction with fractions that have like or unlike denominators

Key Study Points

When two fractions have <u>like denominator</u>, add or subtract the numerator and leave the denominator as it is.

For example, $\frac{1}{9} + \frac{4}{9} = \frac{5}{9}$

When adding with mixed numbers, we can add the integer parts and fraction parts separately.

For example, $2\frac{1}{7} + 1\frac{3}{7} = 2 + \frac{1}{7} + 1 + \frac{3}{7} = 3\frac{4}{7}$

When subtracting with mixed numbers, we can borrow one from the integer parts if the subtrahend has a fraction larger than minuend.

For example, $4\frac{1}{6} - \frac{5}{6} = 3\frac{7}{6} - \frac{5}{6} = 3\frac{2}{6} = 3\frac{1}{3}$

When two fractions have <u>unlike denominator</u>, take these steps:

Step 1: find the common denominator (LCM of original denominators)

Step 2: expand fractions (like comparing fraction)

Step 3: add or subtract the numerator.

Also, remember to simplify your answers.

Worked Examples

Example 1: $\dfrac{5}{12} + \dfrac{2}{9}$

Step 1: find LCM of 12 and 9

LCM of 12 and 9 is 36

Step 2: expand fractions to common denominator

$$\frac{5}{12} = \frac{5 \times 3}{12 \times 3} = \frac{15}{36}$$

$$\frac{2}{9} = \frac{2 \times 4}{9 \times 4} = \frac{8}{36}$$

Step 3: add the numerator.

$$\frac{5}{12} + \frac{2}{9} = \frac{15}{36} + \frac{8}{36} = \frac{15 + 8}{36} = \frac{23}{36}$$

Example 2: $3\dfrac{1}{6} - 1\dfrac{7}{8}$

$$3\frac{1}{6} - 1\frac{7}{8}$$
Find the LCM of 6 and 8

LCM is 24

$$= 3\frac{4}{24} - 1\frac{21}{24}$$
Expand the fractions

$$= 2\frac{28}{24} - 1\frac{21}{24}$$
Since fraction part of subtrahend is larger than fraction part of minuend, borrow 1 from integer

$$= 1\frac{7}{24}$$
Subtract the whole number and numerator

Example 3: $5\dfrac{7}{10} + 2\dfrac{3}{4}$

$$5 + 2 + \frac{7}{10} + \frac{3}{4}$$
Add integer parts and fraction part separately

LCM of 10 and 4 is 20

$$= 7 + \frac{14}{20} + \frac{15}{20}$$
Expand the fractions

$$= 7\frac{29}{20}$$ Add the numerator

$$= 8\frac{9}{20}$$ Change the answer to mixed number

Practice Questions

1. $\frac{2}{9} + \frac{3}{9}$

2. $\frac{5}{12} + \frac{3}{12}$

3. $\frac{13}{10} + \frac{5}{10}$

4. $1\frac{3}{8} + 2\frac{1}{8}$

5. $3\frac{3}{4} + 5\frac{3}{4}$

6. $\frac{6}{7} - \frac{3}{7}$

7. $\frac{9}{14} - \frac{3}{14}$

8. $\frac{32}{15} - \frac{7}{15}$

9. $4\frac{5}{6} - 1\frac{1}{6}$

10. $3\frac{3}{10} - 1\frac{7}{10}$

11. $\frac{8}{15} + \frac{1}{3}$

12. $\frac{7}{10} + \frac{9}{25}$

13. $\frac{13}{18} + \frac{11}{12}$

14. $2\frac{1}{24} + 1\frac{4}{15}$

15. $3\frac{7}{12} + 2\frac{11}{16}$

16. $\frac{7}{10} - \frac{3}{5}$

17. $\frac{9}{14} - \frac{2}{21}$

18. $\frac{22}{27} - \frac{7}{12}$

19. $5\frac{13}{32} - 1\frac{5}{24}$

20. $4\frac{2}{15} - 1\frac{7}{18}$

21. $\frac{3}{18} + \frac{5}{12} - \frac{3}{16}$

22. $\frac{1}{10} + \frac{5}{6} - \frac{4}{15}$

23. $2\frac{1}{15} - 1\frac{7}{9} + 2\frac{19}{30}$

24. $5\frac{8}{21} - 1\frac{16}{35} + 2\frac{5}{6}$

Fractions, Decimals and Percentage

 How can we write $\frac{1}{5}$ as a decimal?

How can we write 0.345 as a fraction?

Section Objectives

- Able to convert between fractions, decimals and percentage
- Know how to compare fractions, decimals and percentage

Key Study Points

<u>Percentage (%) means for every 100</u>. When we see the percentage sign, we can easily change it into a fraction with 100 as its denominator.

For example, $27\% = \frac{27}{100}$

To convert <u>percentage to decimals</u>, we divide the percentage by 100 and we can move the decimal point to the left 2 times.

$$\frac{27}{100} = 27 \div 100 = 0.27 \qquad 0.27$$

To convert <u>decimals to fraction</u>,

For example, 3.65 has 2 decimal places.

① Write 365 as the numerator $\longrightarrow$ $\frac{365}{100} = 3\frac{65}{100} = 3\frac{13}{20}$

② Write 100 as the denominator $\longrightarrow$

because there are two decimal places in 3.65

③ Simplify the fraction

To convert <u>decimals to percentage</u>, we can move the decimal point to the right 2 times and add a percentage sign.

For example, $0.38 = 38\%$

$$0.38 \qquad 0.38\%$$

To convert <u>fraction to decimals</u>, divide the numerator by the denominator.

To convert <u>fraction to percentage</u>, first convert the fraction to decimal and then convert it to percentage.

Worked Examples

Example 1: Convert 426.4% to decimals and fraction.

Move the decimal points to the left 2 times. 426.4% = 4.264

① Write 4264 as the numerator

② Write 1000 as the denominator

because there are 3 decimal places in 4.264

$$\frac{4264}{1000} = 4\frac{264}{1000} = 4\frac{33}{125}$$

③ Simplify the fraction

Example 2: Convert 5.39 to percentage and fraction.

Move the decimal points to the right 2 times. 5.39 = 539%

① Write 539 as the numerator

② Write 100 as the denominator

because there are 2 decimal places in 5.39

$$\frac{539}{100} = 5\frac{39}{100}$$

③ Simplify the fraction

Example 3: Convert $\frac{5}{8}$ to decimals and percentage.

Therefore, $\frac{5}{8} = 0.625$.

Moving the decimal points to the right 2 times.

$0.625 = 62.5\%$

```
                6  2  5
        8 ⟌  5 . 0  0  0
             4   8
            ─────────────
                 2  0
                 1  6
            ─────────────
                    4  0
                    4  0
            ─────────────
```

Practice Questions

Convert the following to decimals and fractions.

1. 55%   4. 213%

2. 89%   5. 576%

3. 24.3%   6. 614.6%

Convert the following to percentages and fractions.

7. 0.3   10. 1.58

8. 0.85   11. 3.96

9. 0.475   12. 15.574

Convert the following to decimals and percentages.

13. $\frac{7}{10}$ 16. $\frac{7}{2}$

14. $\frac{1}{5}$ 17. $4\frac{3}{16}$

15. $\frac{3}{4}$ 18. $3\frac{7}{8}$

Arrange the following from the largest to the least.

19. $\frac{1}{8}$, 0.5, 63%   22. 6.9, $\frac{69}{100}$, 6.9%

20. 2.4%, 0.24, $\frac{1}{4}$ 23. $\frac{1}{5}$, 5, 50%

21. $\frac{1}{3}$, 30%, 0.35   24. 900%, $\frac{9}{2}$, 9.2

Percentage problems

How can we find 20% of 40?

Section Objectives

- Know how to find the percentage of a number
- Able to solve real life problem making use of percentages

Key Study Points

When we need to find the percentage of a number, we use multiplication.

For example, 25% of 32 is 8 because $32 \times 25/100 = 8$

To find what percent of one number is another number, we can put them in a fraction form.
To do it, identify which number represents the whole and which number represents the part.
Put the whole in the denominator and the part in the numerator.

For example,

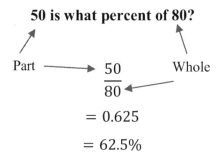

50 is what percent of 80?

Part $\longrightarrow \dfrac{50}{80} \longleftarrow$ Whole

$= 0.625$

$= 62.5\%$

Worked Examples

Example 1: What is 145% of 90?

$90 \times 145\% = 90 \times 1.45 = 130.5$

Remember: when percentage $> 100\%$, the new number will be larger than original number.

Example 2: 150 is what percent of 80?

150 represents part and 80 represents whole. Therefore, 150 is the numerator and 80 is the denominator.

$$\frac{150}{80} = 1.875 = 187.5\%$$

Example 2: There are 30 students in a class. 40% of the class needs glasses. 21 of the students are boys.

(a) How many students need glasses?

$30 \times 40\% = 12$

There are 12 students that need glasses.

(b) What percent of the class is boys?

The whole is the total number of students in class. The part is the number of boys.

$\frac{21}{30} = 0.7 = 70\%$

70% of the class is boys.

Practice Questions

1. What is 30 % 10?
2. What is 20% of 25?
3. What is 64% of 50?
4. What is 40 % of 48?
5. What is 22% of 94?
6. What is 78% of 134?
7. What is 145% of 278?
8. What is 368% of 1070?

9. 5 is what percent of 10?
10. 12 is what percent of 20?
11. 36 is what percent of 50?
12. 25 is what percent of 80?
13. 75 is what percent of 120?
14. 99 is what percent of 300?
15. 60 is what percent of 40?
16. 280 is what percent of 125?

17. There are 25 apples in a crate but 20% of the apples are rotten. How many apples are rotten?

18. There are 400 staff in an office. If 2% of the staff is management, how many managers are there?

19. In a small library, there are 800 books in total. If there are 600 fiction books, what percent of the books are fiction?

20. Jack usually spends 40 hours at work in a week. Last week, he spent 9 hours in total in meetings. What is the percentage of time he spent last week at meetings?

21. In Mrs. Smith's pencil box, there are 26 pencils and 54 crayons. What percentage of box is crayons?

22. In the barn, there are 240 pounds of produce. There are pumpkins, tomatoes and cucumbers.

    (a) If 20% of the produce is pumpkin, how many pounds of pumpkin are there?

    (b) If there are 72 pounds of tomatoes, what is the percentage of tomatoes?

    (c) The farmer decided to bring 45% of the cucumber to the farmer's market, how many pounds of cucumber will be taken to the farmer's market?

23. In a closet, there are 200 pieces of clothing. 25% of the clothing is dresses and 24% are pants. There are 42 jackets in the closet. The rest of the clothing is shirts.

    (a) How many dresses are there in the closet?

    (b) What of clothing is jackets?

    (c) 25% of the pants are jeans. How many pair of jeans are there?

Ratio

 What is the meaning of 1:2?

Section Objectives

- Understand the meaning of ratio
- Able to do basic operations
- Able to solve real life problems with ratios

Key Study Points

Ratio is a way to compare two or more quantities. The ratio of two quantities 'a' and 'b' is denoted by **a : b** (read as 'a is to b').

The order of the quantities matters, i.e., <u>1 : 2 is not the same as 2 : 1</u>.

Remember, ratio is the comparison of two or more quantities. The terms do not necessarily represent the actual quantity.

For example,

In a bag, there are 10 red balls and 20 blue balls. The ratio of number of red balls to the number of blue balls can be written as 1 : 2 or 10 : 20.

Ratio is like fraction in two ways.

1. Ratio remains the same when the terms are divided or multiplied with the same number. For example, 1 : 2 = 2 : 4 because 1 x 2 : 2 x 2 = 2 : 4.

2. Ratio is <u>simplified</u> when there is no common factor for the terms. For example, 2 : 4 can be simplified to 1 : 2 and 1 : 2 is a simplified ratio.

Each of the quantities is called a term. Ratio can be two terms or three term. 1: 2 is a two-term ratio and 2 : 3 : 5 is a three-term ratio.

We can combine two two-term ratios into one three-term ratio if there is a common term in the two two-term ratios. Here are the steps to combine two two-term ratios into one three-term ratio.

Step 1: find the LCM of the quantities of common term

Step 2: expand the two ratios so the common term is the same

Step 3: combine the two ratios

For example, a: b = 2 : 3 and b : c = 4 : 5. Find a: b: c.

Step 1: find the LCM of the quantities of the common term

Since b is the common term in both ratios, we need to find the LCM of 3 and 4. LCM of 3 and 4 is 12.

a : b   = 2 : 3

b : c   = 4 : 5

Step 2: expand the two ratios so the common term is the same

Expand both ratios so the common term in the ratio is 12.

a : b   = 2 x 3 : 3 x 4   = 6 : 12

b: c   = 4 x 3 : 5 x 3   = 12 : 15

Step 3: combine the ratios

a: b : c = 6 : 12 : 15

Worked Examples

Example 1: Simplify 9 : 15 : 30.

3 is the common factor for 9, 15 and 30.

9 : 15 : 30

= 9 ÷ 3 : 15 ÷ 3 : 30 ÷ 3

= 3 : 5 : 6

Example 2: a : b = 14 : 5 and a : c = 7 : 10. Find a : b : c.

Step 1: Find the LCM of 14 and 7.

LCM of 14 and 7 is 14

a : b   = 14 : 5

a : c   = 7 : 10

Step 2: expand the ratio so the common term is 14

a : b = 14 : 5   = 14 : 5

a : c = 7 x 2 :   10 x 2 = 14 : 20

Step 3: combine the ratios

a : b : c = 14 : 5 : 20

Practice Questions

For questions 1 to 8, simplify the ratios.

1. 5 : 15
2. 9 : 21
3. 70 : 49
4. 36 : 81
5. 20 : 40 : 80
6. 85 : 20 : 65
7. 24 : 27 : 32
8. 56 : 28 : 16
9. a : b = 4 : 1 and b : c = 2 : 5. Find a : b : c
10. a : b = 7 : 12 and b : c = 4 : 1. Find a : b : c
11. a : b = 2 : 3 and a : c = 2 : 5. Find a : b : c
12. a : b = 8 : 5 and a : c = 12 : 5. Find a : b : c
13. a : c = 9 : 22 and b : c = 2 : 11. Find a : b : c

14. In a bag, there are 6 red balls and 4 blue balls.

   (a) What is the ratio of the number of red balls to the number of blue balls?

   (b) What is the ratio of the number of blue balls to the total number of balls?

   (c) What is the ratio of the total number of balls to the number of red balls?

15. In a fruit punch, there is 50 ml of lemon juice, 1800 ml of orange juice and 800 ml of water.

   (a) What is the ratio of lemon juice to orange juice?

   (b) What is the ratio of orange juice to water?

   (c) What is the ratio of orange juice to lemon juice to water?

16. In a school, there are 900 students 18 teachers and 4 clerks.

   (a) What is the teacher student ratio in this school?

   (b) What is the ratio of the number of clerks to the number of teachers?

   (c) What is the ratio of the number of all staffs to the number of students?

   (d) If the school wants to raise the teacher student ratio, should they hire more teachers or allow more students to enroll to the school?

Proquartion

 How can we make use of ratio?

Section Objectives

- Understand what proportion is
- Know how to find a quantity with a given ratio

Key Study Points

Proportion are equal ratios.

For example, $3 : 4 = 6 : 8$ or $\dfrac{2}{5} = \dfrac{6}{15}$ shows proportion.

When two ratios are equal, the cross products of the ratio are the same.

For example, $\dfrac{2}{5} = \dfrac{6}{15}$ and $2 \times 15 = 5 \times 6$.

With a given ratio, we can find the unknown quantity using proportion.

For example: If a : b = 2 : 5 and a = 4 find b

$$2 : 5 = 4 : b$$

$$\frac{2}{5} = \frac{4}{b}$$

$$2b = 20$$

$$b = 10$$

When given the total quantities and the ratio, we can find the individual quantity by dividing the total quantity into equal shares and dividing it according to the ratio.

For example:

If $a : b = 5 : 3$ and $a + b = 24$.

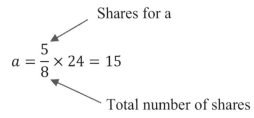

$$a = \frac{5}{8} \times 24 = 15$$

Shares for a

Total number of shares

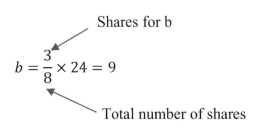

$$b = \frac{3}{8} \times 24 = 9$$

Shares for b

Total number of shares

Worked Examples

Example 1: The standard teacher-student ratio in a school is 1:15.

(a) If a school has 25 teachers, how many students are there in the school?

$$1 : 15 = 25 : x$$

$$\frac{1}{15} = \frac{25}{x}$$

$$x = 25 \times 15 = 375$$

There are 375 students in the school.

(b) If a school has 270 students, how many teachers are there in the school?

$$1 : 15 = x : 270$$

$$\frac{1}{15} = \frac{x}{270}$$

$$15x = 270$$

$$x = 18$$

There are 18 teachers in the school.

Remember to check the order of terms given in the ratio.

Example 2: To make a lemonade, we need 120 ml of water for every 5 ml of lemon juice. If there are 500 ml of lemonade, how much lemon juice and water is added to the lemonade?

Lemon juice in 500ml of lemonade $= \dfrac{5}{120+5} \times 500 = 20\ ml$

Water in 500ml of lemonade $= \dfrac{120}{120+5} \times 500 = 480\ ml$

Practice Questions

For questions 1 to 12, solve for the unknowns.

1. $\dfrac{1}{4} = \dfrac{5}{x}$

2. $\dfrac{5}{6} = \dfrac{10}{x}$

3. $\dfrac{24}{30} = \dfrac{32}{x}$

4. $\dfrac{1}{5} = \dfrac{x}{15}$

5. $\dfrac{5}{8} = \dfrac{x}{24}$

6. $\dfrac{3}{15} = \dfrac{x}{25}$

7. $4 : 1 = x : 16$

8. $1 : 2 = x : 8$

9. $5 : 9 = 25 : x$

10. $2 : 7 = 16 : x$

11. $14 : x = 21 : 6$

12. $x : 12 = 14 : 42$

13. The ratio of boys to girls in a class is 2:3. If there are 16 boys in the class, how many girls are there in the class?

14. On the coffee table, there are 6 magazines and some books. If the ratio of the number of magazines to the number of books is 3 : 5, how many books are there?

15. In the school library, there are some laptop computers and some desktop computers. The ratio of desktop computers to laptop computers is 1 : 7. If there are 14 laptop computers, how many desktop computers are there?

16. The ratio of boys to girls in a school is 3 : 7. If there are 500 students in the school, how many boys are there?

17. According to the recipe, 60 grams of sugar is needed for every 180 grams of flour.

    (a) What is the ratio of weight of sugar to the weight of flour?

    (b) If Lily uses 120 grams of flour in her batter, how much sugar does she need?

    (c) If the weight of sugar and flour is 600 grams, how much flour is used?

18. In the parking lot, the ratio of white cars to black cars to silver cars is 5: 4: 2. If there are a total of 55 cars in the parking lot,

    (a) How many white cars are there in the parking lot?

    (b) After 5 white cars leave the parking lot, what is the new ratio of white cars to black cars to silver cars?

Similar Shapes

 What make two triangles similar?

Section Objectives

- Understand what makes triangles similar
- Able to identify similar shapes
- Know what scale factor is and how to find it
- Able to find side lengths of similar figures

Key Study Points

Two triangles are similar if the <u>corresponding sides are in proportion</u>.

For example,

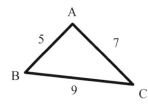 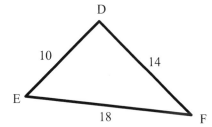

The proportion of corresponding sides are equal for this pair of triangles because

$$\frac{5}{10} = \frac{7}{14} = \frac{9}{18}$$

Since the triangle is similar, we can write $\triangle ABC \sim \triangle DEF$.

Order of the vertex in the statement shows us which vertex/side are corresponding to each other.

For example, vertex A corresponds to vertex D and BC corresponds to EF.

The scale factor is the <u>multiplier</u> for changing the size of the shapes.

For enlargement, scale factor > 1.

For reduction, scale factor < 1.

$$\text{Scale factor} = \frac{\text{corresponding side of new shape}}{\text{corresponding side of original shape}}$$

For example, the scale factor for the above pair of triangles is $\frac{5}{10} = \frac{1}{2}$

To find the side length of similar shapes, we can make use of the proportion of corresponding sides and the scale factor.

Worked Examples

Example 1: If $\triangle BAC \sim \triangle DEF$, find the unknown in the figure.

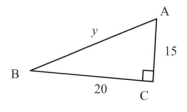 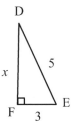

Since $\triangle BAC \sim \triangle DEF$, the corresponding sides are AC and EF, AB and DE, BC and DF.

$$\frac{AC}{EF} = \frac{AB}{DE}$$

$$\frac{15}{3} = \frac{y}{5}$$

$$y = 25$$

$$\frac{AC}{EF} = \frac{BC}{DF}$$

$$\frac{15}{3} = \frac{20}{x}$$

$$15x = 60$$

$$x = 4$$

Example 2: A rectangular photo of dimension 6 cm by 8 cm is resized by a scale factor of $\frac{3}{2}$.

(a) Is the resizing an enlargement or reduction?

Since scale factor is larger than 1, the resizing is an enlargement.

(b) What is the dimension of the resized photo?

The width of the resized photo is $6 \times \frac{3}{2} = 9$ cm

The length of the resized photo is $8 \times \frac{3}{2} = 12$ cm

So, the dimension of the resized photo is 9 cm x 12 cm.

Example 3: The shadow cast by a 6-meter building is 0.9 meter. Find the length of a shadow cast by a 2-meter tall basketball player.

First, draw the figure representing this problem. The shadow and the building make a right-angled triangle.

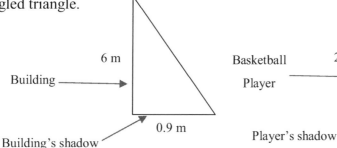

Then, find the player's basketball shadow using proportion.

$$\frac{6}{2} = \frac{0.9}{x}$$

$$6x = 1.8$$

$$x = 0.3$$

So the shadow of the basketball player is 0.3 meter.

Practice Questions

1. $\triangle ABC \sim \triangle DEF$, find x and y.

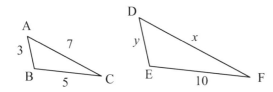

2. $\triangle ABC \sim \triangle DEF$, find x and y.

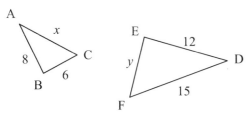

3. $\triangle ABC \sim \triangle FDE$, find x and y.

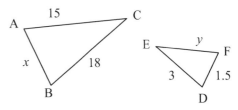

4. $\triangle XYZ \sim \triangle PQR$, find x and y.

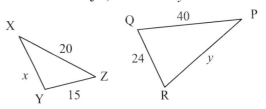

5. The flag pole that is 270 cm tall casts a shadow 180 cm long. The light pole is 240 cm. What is the length of the shadow of the light pole?

6. A 0.8-meter tall garbage can casts a 1-meter shadow. What is the length of the shadow of a 4-meter tall pine tree?

7. John's height is 105 cm and he is walking alongside his father. If John's shadow is 80 cm and his dad's shadow is 144 cm, find the height of his dad.

8. A picture is reduced to a thumbnail for a website by a scale of factor of $\frac{3}{200}$. If the original picture is 600 pixels wide, how wide (measured in pixels) is the thumbnail?

9. A real sports car is 50 meter long. A toy car modeling the sports car is scaled down by a factor of $\frac{1}{80}$. How long (measured in cm) is the toy car?

10. An architect builds a model of a building he designed. The width of the building is 25 cm. If the actual building is 150 times the size of the model, what is the width of the actual building (measured in m)?

11. In Judy's dollhouse, everything is made in proportion to real objects. A chair is only 3 cm tall to model a real chair that is 72 cm tall.

    (a) If someone is to make a real chair modeling the chair in the dollhouse, what is the scale factor?

    (b) If Judy wants to make a towel according to the real towel that is 36 cm wide, what is the scale factor?

    (c) What will be the width of the towel in the dollhouse?

12. Sam drew a map for his neighborhood that is 40 cm by 40 cm. The map is supposed to cover an area of 80 m by 80 m. What is the scale factor of the map?

Using Letters for Unknown Values

 What is the meaning of x + 3 in a real life situation?

Section Objectives

- Understand that letters can be used to represent unknown values
- Know how to represent different arithmetic operations with numbers and letters
- Able to translate sentences into algebraic expressions

Key Study Points

Letters are often used to represent unknown values.

We can use both numbers and letters in our calculations. We treat letters the same way we treat numbers.

For example,

$6 + p$ represents the sum of 6 and p.

$h - 12$ means take away 12 from h.

$3n$ represents the product of 3 and n.

$\dfrac{7}{a}$ means divide 7 into a groups.

We can represent real life situations using the numbers and letters.

For example:

A class has x students. x represents the number of students in the class. It can be 15, 26 or 38 or any other number. We might not know the actual number of students in class.

But if there are 5 more students joining this class, there will be total of $\underline{x + 5}$ students in the class.

Worked Examples

Example 1: Write an algebraic expression for "half of b".

Half means dividing by 2 (or multiplying $\frac{1}{2}$ with b). So, "half of b" can be represented by $\frac{b}{2}$.

Example 2: Write an algebraic expression for "take 10 away from the product of 6 and c".

When the statement indicates more than one operation, we need to pay attention to which number is used in which operations.

Product of 6 and c means $6c$.

Take 10 away indicates subtracting 10 from something.

When we put the two of them together, "take 10 away from the product of 6 and c" can be represented by **$6c - 10$.**

Example 3: Write an algebraic expression for "twice of the difference between k and 8".

Difference between k and 8 can be represented by $k - 8$.

Twice of a value means 2 times the value.

Putting them together we have **$2(k - 8)$.**

Remember to put the brackets around $k - 8$ because we need to find twice the difference between k and 8.

Example 4: Fred is 5 years old. His brother is **r** years older than him. After 4 years, how old will Fred's brother be?

His brother's age now is $5 + r$.

After 4 years, his brother's age will be $5 + r + 4 = \mathbf{9 + r}$

Example 5: The price of a fan was **$e.** There is a big sale in the store and all fans are half priced. Tom has a coupon that will take $5 off the discounted price. What is the price he needs to pay?

Since the fan is half priced, the discounted price is $\frac{e}{2}$.

Together with Tom's coupon, the price will be $\frac{e}{2} - 5$.

Remember according to the description, the $5 will be taken away *after* the price is discounted. So the price that Tom needs to pay is $\frac{e}{2} - 5$ (and not $\frac{e-5}{2}$).

Practice Questions

For questions 1 to 10, write the algebraic expression for the following.

1. Sum of x and 3
2. Subtract 9 from p
3. Multiply 6 and h
4. Divide y by 3
5. Divide the sum of 5 and s by 4
6. Difference between twice of k and 17
7. The quotient of s and 8 decreased by 6
8. Take away 4 from the product of 12 and b
9. One third of f times 5
10. 6 more than the quotient of 14 and m
11. Noah usually goes to work 40 hours a week. Last week, he worked overtime for b hours. How many hours did he work last week?
12. Jack bought 11 packs of chocolate bars. In each pack, there are c bars of chocolate. How many chocolate bars did he buy in total?
13. Ken's height is 163 cm. He grew d cm this past year. What was Ken's height last year?
14. Mike had p pens. He shared his pens with 5 of his friends. How many pens does each friend gets?
15. In the class library, there were 80 books. There are 15 children in the class and they each borrowed r books. How many books were left in the library?

16. The movie ticket for each adult costs *m* pounds and the movie ticket for each child costs 5 pounds. How much does it cost for Josh's parents to go to movie with Josh?

17. The weight of 6 apples is *y* grams. The weight of a watermelon is 884 grams. What is the difference between the weight of the watermelon and an apple?

18. A fiction book has *t* chapters and each chapter is 34 pages. Jane read 126 pages of the book. How many more pages does she have left to read?

Simple Equations

 If $a + 15 = 24$, what does a represent?

Section Objectives

- Understand the concept of simple equations
- Know how to find missing numbers in equations

Key Study Points

Equations says that two things are equal.

For example, $9 + 15 = 24$ is an equation that says $9 + 15$ and 24 is equal.

We can also use letters to represent the unknowns in equation.

For example, $a + 15 = 24$ is an equation that says $a + 15$ and 24 is equal.

If in the equation there is only one unknown, we can find the unknown.

In the above equation $a + 15 = 24$, we know that a represents 9 because $9 + 15 = 24$.

To find the unknown in an equation, we should remember to keep the following in mind.

1. To remove a number, we should use the opposite operation of the original operation
2. We have to do the same operation on both sides to keep the equation remaining equal
3. Leave the unknown on its own

For example,

$$a + 1 = 8$$
$$a + 1 - 1 = 8 - 1 \qquad \text{Subtract 1 from both sides}$$

$$a = 7$$

Worked Examples

Example 1: Find h if $5h = 200$.

$$5h = 200$$

$$\frac{5h}{5} = \frac{200}{5} \qquad\qquad \text{Divide both sides by 5}$$
(original operation is multiplying by 5)

$$h = 40$$

Example 2: Find t if $\frac{t}{3} - 5 = 7$.

$$\frac{t}{3} - 5 = 7$$

$$\frac{t}{3} - 5 + 5 = 7 + 5 \qquad\qquad \text{Add 5 to both sides}$$
(original operation is subtracting 5)

$$\frac{t}{3} = 12$$

$$\frac{t}{3} \times 3 = 12 \times 3 \qquad\qquad \text{Multiply 3 to both sides}$$
(original operation is dividing by 3)

$$t = 36$$

Remember: to leave the unknown on its own, we first remove numbers that are added/subtracted and then remove numbers that are connected by multiplication/division.

Practice Questions

For questions 1 to 12, find the unknowns.

1. $x + 9 = 15$

2. $u - 4 = 10$

3. $6t = 18$

4. $\frac{r}{2} = 9$

5. $4e = 20$

6. $p - 8 = 50$

7. $3 + s = 12$

8. $\frac{w}{7} = 7$

9. $2h + 7 = 15$

10. $\frac{b}{5} - 9 = 1$

11. $4 + \frac{a}{9} = 11$

12. $11 + 6b = 35$

For questions 13 to 20, write an equation for the given situation and find the unknowns.

13. There are b boys in the class and 14 girls in the class. There are total of 35 students in the class.

14. On his birthday, Josh received p presents. He opened 5 of them and there were 4 unopened presents.

15. There are 15 classes in the school. In each class, there are n students. There are total of 270 students in the school.

16. Mrs. Smith had c sheets of color paper and she distributed it to 16 students in her class. Each student gets 5 sheets of color paper for their art project.

17. John's dad is g years old now. John's age is 8 less than third of his dad's age and John is two years old now.

18. Dora bought t pens that cost $4 each and a book that was $15. The total cost of what she bought is $27.

19. Mrs. Joy opens 2 packs of crayons with e crayons in each pack. After she gave 13 crayons to her students, there were 9 crayons left.

20. Grandma made d cupcakes. She put the cupcakes into 6 boxes. Joan ate one whole box of cupcakes. She felt too full because she ate 5 cupcakes.

Formulas

Is it possible to find the unknowns if there is more than one unknown?

Section Objectives

- Understand what formulas are
- Understand what ordered pairs are
- Know that substitution is needed to evaluate a formula
- Able to evaluate the formulas given values of all unknowns except one

Key Study Points

Formulas is an equation that shows us the relationship between two or more quantities.

For example, $P = L + 5$ defines the relationship between Linda's age and Paul's age because Paul is 5 years older than Linda.

When there are 2 or more unknowns, there are different possibilities for the values of the unknowns that can fit into the formula.

For example, since Paul is 5 years older than Linda, Paul is 15 years old when Linda is 10 years old. There are endless possibilities for Linda and Paul's age.

For $P = L + 5$:

If L is 6, P is 11.

If L is 3, P is 9.

If L is 47, P is 52.

The list goes on. These pairs of possible values are called <u>ordered pairs</u>.

We can find one quantity when the other quantity (or quantities) is (or are) given. To find the unknown quantity, we need to <u>substitute the given quantities into the formula</u>.

For example, to find Paul's age, we need to know Linda's age.

When Linda is 20 years old, we can substitute 20 for L.

So then, $P = 20 + 5 = 25$. When Linda is 20, Paul is 25.

When Linda's age is different, Paul's age will change accordingly.

A formula can have more than 2 quantities.

For example, $P = 2(w + l)$ is the formula for perimeter of rectangles and it has 3 unknown quantities: perimeter, width and length.

To find perimeter of rectangles, we need the values for its width and length.

If the width and length of a rectangle is 6 units and 9 units, we can find its perimeter by substituting the values of its width and length into the formula.

$$P = 2(w + l) = 2(6 + 9) = 2(15) = 30$$

When the width and length of a rectangle is 6 units and 9 units, the perimeter is 30 units.

Worked Examples

Example 1: Find 4 ordered pairs for the formula $H = \frac{e}{3}$.

To find the ordered pairs, we can substitute values into the place of e and find the corresponding values of H.

When $e = 15$, $H = \frac{15}{3} = 5$.

When $e = 21$, $H = \frac{21}{3} = 7$.

When $e = 39$, $H = \frac{39}{3} = 13$.

When $e = 300$, $H = \frac{300}{3} = 100$.

The 4 ordered pairs are

$e = 15$ and $H = 5$, $e = 21$ and $H = 7$, $e = 39$ and $H = 13$, $e = 300$ and $H = 100$

Example 2: Given $C = 4x + r$, find C if $x = 6, r = 2$.

$$C = 4x + r = 4(6) + 2 = 24 + 2 = 26$$

C is 26 if $x = 6, r = 2$.

Example 3: Michael has \$x and he is going to buy y books that are \$4 each.

(a) Write a formula to find the money he would have left (M) with unknowns x and y.

The money Michael would have left will be equal to the original amount of money minus the cost of the books. The money that he spends on the book would be determined by the number of books multiplied by 4 (which is 4y).

Therefore, the formula is **M = x – 4y.**

(b) Find the money he would have left (M) if he has \$50 originally and is going to buy 7 books.

Substitute 50 in the place of x and 7 in the place of y to find M.

$M = 50 - 4\,(7) = 22$

Michael has \$22 left if he has \$50 originally and is going to buy 7 books.

Practice Questions

1. Find 3 ordered pairs for the formula $A = 26 - n$.

2. Find 3 ordered pairs for the formula $R = 5d$.

3. Given $T = 6 + d$, find T if
   (a) $d = 4$
   (b) $d = 9$

4. Given $M = f - 14$, find M if
   (a) $f = 60$
   (b) $f = 22$

5. Given $a = v + k$, find a if
   (a) $v = 7, k = 9$

   (b) $v = 18, k = 36$

6. Given $N = 6d - T$, find N if
   (a) $d = 5, T = 2$
   (b) $d = 3, T = 7$

7. Given $E = \frac{R}{6}$, find E if
   (a) $R = 12$
   (b) $R = 4$

8. Given $A = \frac{Q}{5} + f$, find E if
   (a) $Q = 15, f = 7$
   (b) $Q = 25, f = 16$

9. The outdoor temperature is 4 degrees higher than indoor.
   (a) Write the formula for the temperature outdoor (T) and the temperature indoor (I).
   (b) Find the temperature outdoor if the temperature indoor is 26 degrees.
   (c) Find the temperature outdoor if the temperature indoor is 4 degrees.

10. Each box contains 8 cookies.
    (a) Write the formula for the total number of cookies (C) and the number of boxes (b).
    (b) Find the total number of cookies if there are 9 boxes.
    (c) Find the total number of cookies if there are 21 boxes.

11. A school needs to hire a teacher for every 20 students enrolled in the school.
    (a) Write the formula for the number of teachers needed (T) and the number of students enrolled in the school (S).

(b) Find the number of teachers needed when there are 280 students enrolled.

(c) Find the number of teachers needed when there are 740 students enrolled.

12. To wrap a present, Lily needs 26 cm of ribbons.

   (a) Write the formula for the total length of ribbons (r) she needs and the number of presents (P) to be wrapped.

   (b) Find the length of ribbons she needs to wrap 9 presents.

   (c) Find the number of presents she needs to wrap 23 presents.

13. The party hall rental cost $50 to rent and the food costs $4 for each guest.

   (a) Write the formula for the total cost (C) and number of guest (g).

   (b) Find the total cost if there are 16 guests.

   (c) Find the total cost if there are 36 guests.

14. Each office can fit 12 clerks in each room. The office also hired some receptionists.

   (a) Write the formula for the total number of staff (S) in the office, number of rooms (r) and the number of receptionists hired (h).

   (b) Find the total number of clerks in the office if there are 5 rooms and 3 receptionists.

   (c) Find the total number of clerks in the office if there are 8 rooms and 6 receptionists.

15. Sean makes $8 per hour during day shift and $14 per hour during night shift.

   (a) Write the formula for Sean's total salary (S), number of hours worked during day shifts (d) and the number of hours worked during night shifts he worked (n).

   (b) Find his total salary if he worked for 11 hours during day shifts and 15 hours during night shifts.

   (c) Find his total salary if he worked for 35 hours during day shifts and 24 hours during night shifts.

Number Sequences

 What is a number sequence?

Section Objectives

- Understand what number sequences are
- Know the rules for given number sequences
- Able to find the missing terms or next terms of number sequence

Key Study Points

Number sequence is a list of numbers in a certain order.

For example, 1, 3, 5, 7, 9 … is a number sequence that contains odd numbers in an ascending order.

The terms in a number sequence are put together using the same rule between the consecutive terms. We can usually find the rule of the sequence by looking for the differences between consecutive terms. Making use of this rule we can find the next term of the number sequence.

For example,

For the sequence 1, 4, 7, 10 … The rule is +3 since

$1 + 3 = 4$ $4 + 3 = 7$ $7 + 3 = 10$

To find the next term, we can apply the rule +3 to 10.

Since $10 + 3 = 13$, the next term is 13.

Remember, the rule of a sequence should be able to apply to <u>all terms</u> in the number sequence.

For example, 5, 10, 15, 21… is not a number sequence as the rule +5 does not apply to all term as the difference between 15 and 21 is 6 instead of 5.

In some cases, the rules of the number sequence are more difficult to find as the differences between each term are different.

For example, in the following sequence, the difference between the terms are different but the differences themselves form a number sequence.

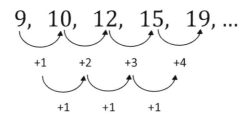

Worked Examples

Example 1: Find the next term of the number sequence 8, 6, 4, 2…

To find the rule, we can first try to find the difference between the consecutive terms.

$6 - 8 = -2$

So, the rule is –2 (not +2 as the list is going down)

The next term in the sequence is 0 because $2 - 2 = 0$.

Example 2: Determine if $4, 3\frac{1}{2}, 2\frac{1}{2}, 1\frac{1}{2}, \ldots$ is a number sequence.

The difference between the first two terms is $4 - 3\frac{1}{2} = \frac{1}{2}$

The difference between the second and third terms is $3\frac{1}{2} - 2\frac{1}{2} = 1$

The difference between the third and fourth terms is $2\frac{1}{2} - 1\frac{1}{2} = 1$

Since the difference between consecutive terms are not the same throughout the sequence, and there are no other patterns, it is not a number sequence.

Example 3: Find the next term for the sequence of 1, 4, 9, 16, 25, …

We can first try to find the difference between different terms.

$$1, \quad 4, \quad 9, \quad 16, \, 25, \, \dots$$

+3   +5   +5   +9

If the difference between terms are not the same, we can look for other pattern in the sequence.

The numbers are all square numbers. Rewriting the number sequence as below;

$$1^2, \quad 2^2, \quad 3^2, \quad 4^2, \quad 5^2, \dots$$

The difference between the bases is +1.

$$1^2, \quad 2^2, \quad 3^2, \quad 4^2, \quad 5^2, \dots$$

+1   +1   +1   +1

Therefore, the next term of the sequence is $6^2 = 36$.

Example 4: Find the missing terms in the number sequence 2, _____ , _____ , 11.

Since the difference between consecutive terms must be the same, we can find the difference between the given terms and divide it among the terms.

The difference between the first term and fourth term is $11 - 2 = 9$

$$2 \quad ? \quad ? \quad 11$$

As there are 2 terms between 2 and 11, the difference of 9 will be divided equally among the three "hops". Therefore, the rules for this number sequence is +3.

The missing terms are $2 + 3 = 5$ and $5 + 3 = 8$.

Practice Questions

For questions 1 to 8, find the next term for the following number sequences.

1. 5, 9, 13, …

2. 10, 6, 2, –2, …

3. 12, 32, 52, 72, …

4. –8, –1, 6, 13, …

5. $3\frac{1}{2}, 4\frac{1}{2}, 5\frac{1}{2}, \ldots$

6. $\frac{1}{2}, \frac{1}{4}, 0, -\frac{1}{4}, \ldots$

7. 9.4, 7.9, 6.4, 4.9, …

8. $-8.5, -6.1, -3.7, -1.3, \ldots$

For questions 9 to 14, determine if the following are number sequence.

9. 3, 6, 9, 12, 15, …

10. 1, 2, 4, 8, 16, …

11. 56, 67, 78, 89, …

12. 3.3, 3.95, 4.6, 5.25, …

13. 4, –4, –8, –12, …

14. $3\frac{1}{3}, 3\frac{2}{3}, 4, 4\frac{1}{3}, \ldots$

For questions 15 to 20, find the missing terms in the number sequence.

15. 5, _____, _____, 17, …

16. 11, _____, _____, 35, _____, …

17. 9.7, _____, 6.3, …

18. $\frac{1}{5}$, _____, _____, $1\frac{2}{5}$, …

19. –5, _____, 5, _____, _____, …

20. $-\frac{1}{10}$, _____, _____, $-3\frac{1}{10}$, …

21. At a performance, the choir is standing in the following pattern: 6 singers at the first row, 11 singers at the second row and 16 singers at the third row. How many singers will be on the fourth row and fifth row?

22. Jenny is training for a marathon race. She starts to train from running 400 meters during a training. The distance she runs increased by 250 meters for every training. How long is she going to run during her 6th practice?

23. Andy made some patterns with marbles. The first three patterns are shown below.

First pattern

Second pattern

Third pattern

(a) What is the rule of the pattern of number of marbles used?

(b) What will be the number of marbles used in the fifth pattern?

24. James built a tower using bricks. There were 6 layers of bricks stacked on top of each other. On the top layer, there were 4 bricks. On second layer, there were 10 bricks. On the third layer, there were 16 bricks. If the pattern goes on,

(a) How many bricks were there on the fourth layers?

(b) How many bricks were used altogether?

25. In an experimenter, a temperature of a solution is decreased by 2.3 degrees Celsius for every minute. At the beginning of the experiment, the temperature of the solution is 18.4 degrees Celsius.

(a) At the end of the second minute, what is the temperature of the solution?

(b) When will the temperature of the solution reach 0 degree Celsius?

26. Peggy decides to start saving some of her pocket money on the first day of November. She started with $\frac{1}{2}$ pound and increased her daily saving by $\frac{1}{4}$ pound.

(a) How much did she save on 4th of November?

(b) How much can she save during the first week of November altogether?

Time

 Which movie is longer, a 140-minute movie or a 2-hour movie?

Section Objectives

- Understand the concept of analogue and digital 12- and 24-hour clocks
- Able to convert different units of time
- Able to do basic arithmetic operation with time
- Know how to find the duration with given start and end time or vice versa
- Know how to find the start or end time given the duration

Key Study Points

There are two ways of representing time. For 12-hour format, twenty-four hours around the clock is divided into a.m. and p.m. Midnight to noon is a.m. and after noon is p.m. And for 24-hour format, time goes from 0:00 (midnight) to 23:59. So, if we see any time larger than 12:00 for 24-hour format, it means it is in the afternoon. For example, 14:00 is 2:00 p.m.

Here are the different units of time and conversion rules for them.

1 minute = 60 seconds   1 day = 24 hours

1 hour = 60 minutes   1 week = 7 days

To convert a smaller unit to a larger unit, we should use multiplication. To convert a larger unit to smaller unit we should use division.

For example, 4 days have 5760 minutes because $4 \times 24 \times 60 = 5760$

When we are doing arithmetic operation with time, remember to align the times according to units. When the unit of the minuend is too small, borrow from a larger unit.

For example

6 h 5 min 46 sec – 3 h 7 min 58 sec

= 6 h 4 min 106 sec – 3 h 7 min 58 sec (change 6 h 5 min 46 sec into 6 h 4 min 106 sec)

= 5 h 64 min 106 sec – 3 h 7 min 58 sec (change 6 h and 4 min into 5 h 64 min)

= 2 h 57 min 48 sec

The usual practice is to express your final answer <u>using the largest unit possible</u>.

For example,

4 min 34 sec × 6

= 24 min 204 sec

= 27 min 24 sec (convert the answer so that we are using minutes as much as possible in the answer)

Here is the relationships between start time, end time and duration.

End time – start time = duration

End time – duration = start time

Start time + duration = end time

For example,

The duration between 9:15 and 14:30 is 5 hours and 15 minutes since 14:30 – 9:15 = 5:15

If the duration crosses over noon/midnight, we can find the duration from the start time to noon/midnight and the noon/midnight to the end time.

For example, we can find the duration between 7:50 a.m. to 4:35 p.m. separating the duration into two:

1. The duration from 7:50 a.m. to noon: 12:00 – 7:50 = 4 hours 10 minutes.
2. The duration from noon to 4:35 p.m. = 4 hours 35 minutes.

Therefore, the total duration from 7:50 a.m. to 4:35 p.m. is

4 hours 10 minutes + 4 hours 35 minutes = 8 hours 45 minutes

Worked Examples

Example 1: The record of a marathon race is 2 hours 54 minutes 14 seconds.

(a) Convert the record into seconds.

2 hours 54 minutes 14 seconds

$= 2 \times 60 \times 60 + 54 \times 60 + 14 = 10{,}454$ seconds

(b) Rita can run 1 km in 4 minutes. If the marathon race is 42 km and Rita can keep her speed for the whole race, can she beat the record of the race?

4 min×42 = 168 minutes = 2 hour 48 minutes

She can beat the record of the race.

Example 2: Joe's meeting started at 11:25 a.m. and ended at 3:45 p.m.

(a) What was the duration of the meeting?

Before noon: 12:00 – 11:25 = 35 minutes

After noon: 3 hour 45 minutes

The duration of meeting is 35 minutes + 3 hour 45 minutes = 4 hours 20 minutes

(b) Joe's work day lasts for 8 hours and 30 minutes. He complained that the meeting took up half of his work day. Is that correct?

8 hour 30 minutes ÷2 = 4 hour 15 minutes

Therefore, he is correct. The meeting too up more than half of his work day.

Practice Questions

For questions 1 to 4, fill in the blanks.

1. 5 minutes 51 seconds = _____ seconds

2. 3 hours 42 minutes = _____ minutes

3. $2\frac{1}{3}$ days = _____ hours

4. $7\frac{5}{12}$ hours = _____ seconds

For questions 5 to 8, simplify these expressions.

5. 15 hours 56 minutes + 13 hours 22 minutes

6. 2 hours 45 seconds – 17 minutes 39 seconds

7. 5 hours 14 minutes 33 seconds × 5

8. 8 hours 21 minutes 9 seconds ÷ 3

9. Ted usually spends 8 hours a night sleeping.

    (a) Convert his sleeping time to minutes

    (b) If there are 28 days in a month, his total sleeping time in a month is equal to how many days?

10. It took Chris 4 hours 13 minutes to drive from his house to his friend's house.

    (a) Convert the driving time to minutes.

    (b) On his way going back to his house, it took him 39 minutes less than the way there. How much did it take him to drive back?

11. Ella spent 15 minutes 35 seconds to finish the first page of the math test and spent 22 minutes 45 seconds to finish the second page of the math test. How much time did she spend on finishing the two pages of the math test?

12. Dan ran 8 laps. If it took him 3 minute 24 seconds for each lap, how much time did he spend running in total?

13. It took Nora 4 hours 35 minutes 3 seconds to finish a race. The winner finished the race in 2 hours 45 minutes 37 seconds. How much faster is the winner?

14. A factory paints 6 cars in 3 hour and 24 minutes. How long does it take to paint one car?

15. On Monday, Molly arrived at work at 9:15 a.m. and left work at 5:25 p.m. How much time did she spend at work?

16. The movie started at 14:05 and ended at 16:20. How long was the movie?

17. The museum opens for 9.5 hours on Fridays. If the museum opens at 10:15 a.m., when does the museum close?

18. Jack's piano lesson is 70 minutes. If his lesson ends at 14:35, when does the lesson starts?

19. It takes the bus 4 hours 35 minutes to arrive at its destination. The bus was scheduled to leave the bus terminal at 11:50 a.m. but left 45 minutes later than scheduled. When did the bus arrived at its destination?

20. A plane left a city at 22:40, which is 20 minutes earlier than the schedule. The plane arrived at its destination at 10:45 the next morning, which is 50 minutes later than schedule. What is the duration of flight according to the schedule?

Weight

 Last week, my bunny weighed 900g and this week it weighed 1 kg. Is my bunny gaining weight?

Section Objectives

- Able to convert weights with different units
- Able to compare different weights
- Able to do arithmetic operations with weights

Key Study Points

The common units for weights are grams (g) and kilograms (kg).

1000 g = 1 kg

When converting kg to gram, we multiply by 1000.

For example, 2.3 kg = 2.3 × 1000g = 2300 g

When converting gram to kg, we divide the weight by 1000.

For example, 358 g = 358 ÷ 1000 kg = 0.358 kg

Here are the weights of some common objects.

The weight of a paper clip is about a gram.

The weight of a 20-cents coin is 20 grams.

The weight of a liter bottle of water is about 1 kg.

When we are doing arithmetic operations with weights, the usual practice is to express your final answer using the larger unit (kg) if possible.

For example, 940 g × 15 = 14100 g = 14.1 kg

When the units of two weights are different, change them into the same unit.

For example, 4 kg 200 g – 1 kg 700 g = 4.2 kg – 1.7 kg = 2.5 kg

Similarly, we can change the weights into the same units and compare them.

For example, which one is heavier? 5.4 kg or 4800 grams?

We can either change both weights to *kg* or *g* to compare them.

5.4 kg = 5400g

So, 5.4 kg is heavier than 4800 grams.

Practice Questions

1. Convert 4500 g into kg.
2. Convert 361 g into kg.
3. Convert 5 kg into grams.
4. Convert 1.7 kg into grams.
5. Convert 0.082 kg into grams.

   For questions 6 to 9, simplify the expressions.

6. 3 kg 750 g + 2 kg 800 g
7. 2 kg – 350 g
8. 370 g × 9
9. 1kg 371 g ÷ 3
10. Grandma has 400 g of all-purpose flour and 0.8 kg of cake flour. Which type of flour weighs more?
11. A kitten weighs 0.9 kg and a puppy weighs 1280 gram. Which one is heavier?
12. The chef has two bags of flour in the kitchen. The bigger bag weighs 2.6 kg and the smaller bag weighs 650 grams. How much flour does he have in total?
13. Oliver has 3 boxes of cereal. If each box of cereal weighs 460 grams, how much cereal does he have in total?

14. Each batch of cookies requires 150 grams of sugar. With 0.75 kg sugar at home, how many batches of cookies can Emily make?

15. Jack's weight is 46.7 kg at the end of this month. He gained 1240 grams this month. What was his weight last month?

16. There were three sticks of butter in the fridge which were 250 g each. May used 0.48 kg of butter to make some muffin. How much butter was left in the fridge?

17. A rabbit weighed 360 g at birth. During the first week, its weight was doubled. During the second to fourth week, it gained 0.4 kg every week. What was the rabbit's weight when it is one month old?

18. A box of candies contained 12 packs of candies with the total weight of 0.9 kg. Andy opened a pack of candies and ate some candies. If there were 42 grams of candies left in the pack, how many grams of candies did Andy eat?

19. Dan bought 420 grams of sugar yesterday and bought another pack of sugar that weighs 730 grams. According to the recipe he is using, he needs 1kg of sugar. Does he have enough sugar?

20. Ben bought 4 bags of apples that weighs 0.35 kg each. He is making three apple pies. Each apple pie needs 700 grams of apples. Does he have enough apples?

Volume

 Is there enough milk in the carton for four children to have breakfast?

Section Objectives

- Able to convert volumes with different units
- Able to compare different volumes
- Able to do arithmetic operations with volumes

Key Study Points

Volume is the capacity of a container.

The common units for volumes are milliliter (mL) and liter (L).

$1000 \text{ mL} = 1 \text{ L}$

When converting L to mL, we multiply by 1000.

For example, $4.1 \text{ L} = 4.1 \times 1000 \text{ mL} = 4100 \text{ mL}$

When converting mL to L, we divide by 1000.

For example, $570 \text{ mL} = 570 \div 1000 \text{ L} = 0.57 \text{ L}$

Here are the volumes of some common containers.

A teaspoon can hold about 5 mL of liquid.

A standard sized coffee mug holds about 250 mL.

So, four mugs can make up about 1 L.

When we are doing arithmetic operations with mL, the usual practice is to express your final answer <u>using the larger unit (L) if possible</u>.

For example, 270 mL × 28 = 7560 mL = 7.56 L

When the units of two volumes are different, change them into the same unit.

For example, 3 L + 5200 mL = 3L + 5.2 L = 8.2 L

Similarly, we can change the volumes into same units and compare them.

For example, which volume is greater? 1.4 L or 1700 mL?

We can either change both to L or mL to compare them.

1.4 L = 1400 mL

So, 1700 mL is greater than 1.4 L.

Practice Questions

1. Convert 560 mL into L.

2. Convert 3580 mL into L.

3. Convert 1.64 L into mL.

4. Convert 0.08 L into mL.

   Simply the expressions.

5. 1.7 L + 240 mL

6. 5 L – 3605 mL

7. 468 mL × 16

8. 3 L 990 mL ÷ 7

9. In the fridge, there was 215 mL of coffee cream. Joe bought a box of coffee cream that is 0.85 L. How much coffee cream is there in total?

10. In the water bottle, there was 1.4 L of water. After Charlie drank 240 ml of water, how much water was left?

11. Ben bought a tray of 12 bottles of water. Each bottle is 350 mL. How much water is there in total?

12. If each glass can hold 200 mL, how many glasses can we fill up with 2.4 L of juice?

13. Judy made a fruit punch with mixed fruit, soda and juice. She used three cans of mixed fruit which is 235 mL each. Four cans of soda which is 355 mL each. At last, she added 2.3 L of juice. How much fruit punch did she make?

14. Ken opened 3 cans of soup and poured them into a saucepan. Each can of soup is 453 mL and the saucepan can hold up to 2.8 L. How much more can the saucepan hold?

15. A chef opened a can of 3.75 L of oil. She poured 950 mL into the fryer. Then, she divided the rest of the oil into 4 bottles. How much oil was in each bottle?

16. The bath tub holds 120 L of water. The shower uses 950 ml of water every minute. If it takes Chris 15 minutes to finish his shower. How much water can he save if he takes a shower instead of a bath?

17. The capacity of a sink is 23.4 L. If the tap is on and filling the sink at the speed of 450 mL every minute, how long does it take to overflow the sink?

18. A carton of milk is 0.976 L and a small box of milk is 235 mL. If the price of four boxes of milk and a carton of milk is the same, which one has better value?

19. A small bottle of juice of 500 mL costs $1.80 and a bigger bottle of juice of 1L costs $3. Which one has better value?

20. Sophia is preparing for a dinner party with 12 guests. Each soup bowl holds 350 mL. Can Sophia use a pot that can hold 4 L to make the soup?

Length

 Anna ran 1.4 km and Jason ran 2320 m. Who ran more?

Section Objectives

- Able to convert lengths with different units
- Able to compare different lengths
- Able to do arithmetic operations with lengths

Key Study Points

The common units for lengths are millimeters (mm), centimeters (cm), meters (m) and kilometers (km). The larger units (m or km) can also be used for distance.

10 mm = 1 cm

100 cm = 1 m

1000 m = 1 km

When converting from a larger unit to a smaller unit, we multiply by 10, 100 or 100.

For example, 3 m = 3 × 100 cm = 300 cm

When converting from a smaller unit to a larger unit, we divide by 10, 100 or 100.

For example, 59 mm = 59 ÷ 10 cm = 5.9 cm

When we are doing arithmetic operations with lengths, the usual practice is to express your final answer <u>using the largest unit (km) and smallest numbers of decimal places if possible</u>.

For example, 30 mm × 144 = 4320 mm = 432 cm = 4.32 m = 0.00432 km

Among these answers, 432 cm and 4.32 m are both reasonable.

When the units of two lengths are different, change them into the same unit.

For example, 3 m – 804 mm = 300 cm – 80.4 cm = 219.6 cm

Similarly, we can change the lengths into same units and compare them.

For example, which one is longer? 1.3 m or 1500 mm?

We can change both lengths to *m, cm* or *mm* to compare them.

1.3 m = 130 cm

1500 mm = 150 cm

So, 1500 mm is longer than 1.3 m.

Practice Questions

1. Convert 21.5 cm into mm.

2. Convert 0.76 m into mm.

3. Convert 378 mm into cm.

4. Convert 0.078 km into cm.

5. Convert 1.05 km into m.

6. Convert 9500 mm into m.

7. Convert 1469 m into km.

8. Convert 2591 cm into km.

    For questions 9 to 12, simplify the expressions.

9. 4.88 km + 1547 m

10. 50 cm – 78 mm

11. 351 m × 7

12. 23 cm ÷ 50

13. A book shelf is 2.3 meters wide. A door is 89 cm wide. Which one is wider?

14. Brian biked for 4.3 km and ran for 540 m. Did he run more or bike more?

15. The bedroom door is 60 mm thick and the front door is 8.6 cm thick. Which one is thicker?

16. A birch tree is 3.69 m, and the pine tree is 49 cm taller than the birch tree. How tall is the pine tree?

17. The shallow end of a swimming pool is 80 cm deep. The deep end of the swimming pool is 5.3 meters deep. What is the difference between the depth of the shallow end and deep end?

18. It took a worker 16 hours to paint a fence that is 10 meters long. How much fence can the worker paint in an hour?

19. Each roll of tape is 87 cm long. Debbie has 4 rolls of tapes. What is the length of the tape in total?

20. Each volume of the encyclopedia is 56 mm thick. If there are 15 volumes, how thick is the whole set of encyclopedias?

21. The flowerbed is 5.4 meter long. A snail starts crawling from one side to the other side and its speed is 45 mm every minute. How long does it take the snail to arrive at the other side?

22. Each lap is 400 m. Jack ran 8 laps. How long did Jack run?

23. Calvin finished a hiking trail in three hours. The trail is 9.8 km long. In the first hour, he hiked for 3.9 km. In the second hour, he took a longer break and only walked for 960 meters. What was the distance he hiked in the third hour?

Angles

How do angles form?
How can we find the size of an angle?

Section Objectives

- Able to name the different parts that make up an angle and name the angle
- Able to identify different types of angles (acute, right, obtuse, straight, reflex and full angles)
- Know how to measure an angle using degrees

Key Study Points

Angles are formed when two lines meet at a common point. The two lines are called arms and the common point is called vertex. We name the angle by the points of the line. The angle shown below can be referred as ∠ABC or ∠CBA. (Remember that the vertex is in the middle)

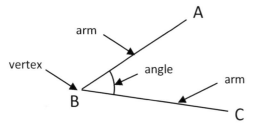

The size of angles is measured by degrees (°).

To measure an angle, we can use the protractor using these steps.

Step 1: Line up the vertex and one of the arms with the base and center of protractor

Step 2: Note the readings on the other arm

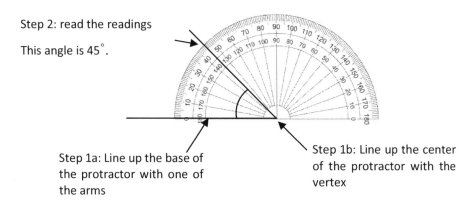

Step 2: read the readings

This angle is 45°.

Step 1a: Line up the base of the protractor with one of the arms

Step 1b: Line up the center of the protractor with the vertex

These are the different types of angles and their measures.

Acute angle – smaller than 90 °

Right angle – 90 °

Obtuse angle – larger than 90 ° and smaller than 180°

Straight angle – 180°

Reflex angle – larger than 180 ° and smaller than 360 °

Round angle – 360 °

A few important rules to remember about angles.

Adjacent angles on a straight line add up to 180 degrees.

Vertically opposite angles have the same measure.

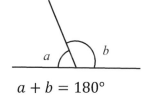

$$a + b = 180°$$

$$a = b$$

Angles at a point sum up to 360 degrees.

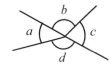

$$a + b + c + d = 180°$$

Worked Examples

Example 1: Identify what types of angles are there inside this shape.

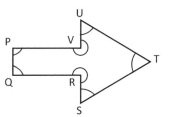

There are three types of angle.

Acute angles (smaller than 90˚): ∠UTS

Right angles (90˚): ∠PQR, ∠QPV

Obtuse angles (larger than 90 ˚ and smaller than 180˚) : ∠PVU, ∠QRS

Example 2: Find the measure of the unknown angle.

$$y + 39° + 56° = 180°$$
$$y = 85°$$

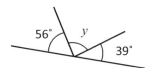

Practice Questions

For questions 1 to 6, name the angles, find its measures and identify its type.

(Use a protractor)

1.

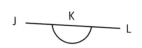

2.

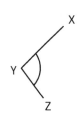

3.

4.
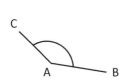

5.

6.

For the questions below, classify which types of angle it is.

7. The smaller angle between the two hands of the clock when it is 3:00.

8. The bigger angle between the two hands of the clock when it is 7:45.

9. The smaller angle between the two hands of the clock when it is 1:10.

10. The bigger angle between the two hands of the clock when it is 6:11.

For questions 11 to 16, find the unknowns in the figure.

11.
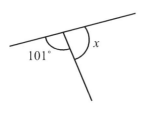

12.
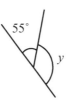

13.
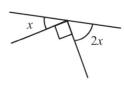

14.
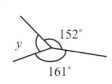

15.

16.
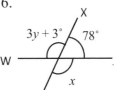

17. What is the measure of the angle travelled by the minute hand for a five-minute interval?

18. What is the measure of the angle between the hour hand and minute hand when the time is (a) 10:00? (b) 10:30?

Circles

 What makes circle different from other shapes?

Section Objectives

- Able to identify different parts of a circle
- Know how to find the area and perimeter of a circle

Key Study Points

The middle of a circle is called the center of the circle.

All the points on the circle are at the same distance from the center.

Radius is the distance from the center to the circle.

Diameter is the line across the circle that passes through the center.

Diameter = 2 × Radius

Circumference is the perimeter of a circle.

Circumference = 2 × π × radius

(The symbol π is called pi and denotes the ratio of the
Circumference of a circle and its diameter.

π = 22/7 which approximately equals 3.14)

Area of a circle is defined by

Area = π × Radius × Radius

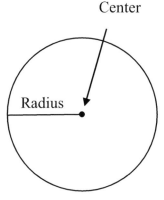

Worked Examples

Example 1: Find the diameter of the circle.

The figure shows the length of the radius of the circle.

Diameter = 2 × 4 cm = 8 cm

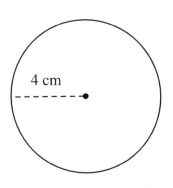

Example 2: Find the circumference and area of the circle.

Since the diameter of the circle is 18 m, the radius is 9 m.

The circumference = 3.14×18 cm = 56.52 cm

The area = 3.14×9 cm $\times 9$ cm = 254.34 cm^2

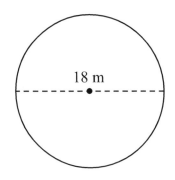

Practice Questions

For questions 1 to 4, find the radius of a circle with the given diameter.

1. 6 cm
2. 20 m
3. 1 km
4. 31.5 mm

For questions 5 to 8, find the diameter of a circle with the given radius.

5. 4 m
6. 26 km
7. 3 mm
8. 2.18 cm

Triangles

 How to find the area of a triangle?

Section Objectives

- Able to identify different types of triangles
- Able to find the areas and perimeters of triangles
- Know how to solve problem involving angles in a triangle

Key Study Points

Triangles are shapes with three sides and three angles. The three angles always sump up to 180 degrees.

These are the types of triangles that are related to the number of equal sides.

Equilateral triangle	Isosceles triangle	Scalene triangle
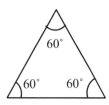	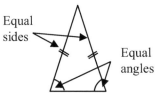	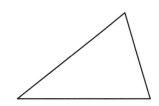
3 equal sides	2 equal sides	no equal sides
3 equal angles	2 equal angles	no equal angles

These are types of triangles that are related to the type of angles in the triangle.

Right triangle	Acute triangle	Obtuse triangle

There is one right angle (90°)	All angles are acute angles.	There is one obtuse angle.

Perimeter of a triangle is the sum of the length of all three sides.

Area of a triangle is $\frac{1}{2} \times base \times height$

Height is the line from one of the three vertices to the opposite side and height must be perpendicular to one of the sides of the triangle.

Worked Examples

Example 1: Identify what type of triangle that ΔABC is.

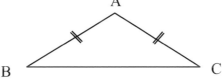

Since AB = AC, ΔABC is an isosceles triangle.

∠A is an obtuse angle. ΔABC is also an obtuse triangle.

Example 2: Find the area and perimeter of the triangle.

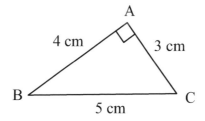

Perimeter = 3 cm + 4 cm + 5 cm = 12 cm

Before we find the area, it is important to identify which sides are the base and height. (Note that base and height are perpendicular to each other).

Remember, the side at the bottom (in this case BC) is not always necessarily the base.

AC and AB are perpendicular to each other, so we can use them to calculate the area of the triangle.

The area $= \frac{1}{2} \times 3 \times 4 = 6$ cm^2

Practice Questions

For questions 1 to 6, identify the types of triangles.

1.

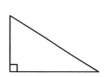

2.

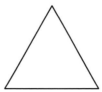

3.

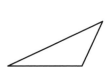

4.

5.

6.

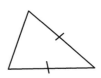

For questions 7 to 12, find the perimeter and the area of these triangles. (All Lengths in cm)

7.

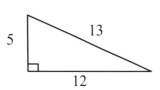

8.

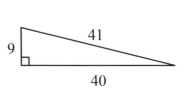

9.

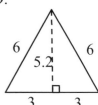

10.

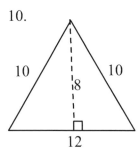

11.

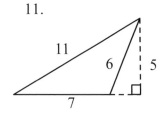

12.

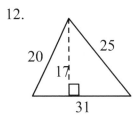

For questions 13 to 18, find the unknowns.

13.

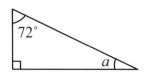

14.

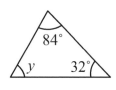

15.

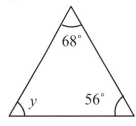

16.

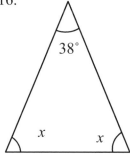

17.

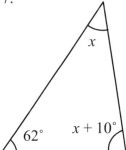

18.

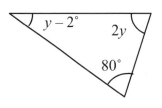

19. Charlie draws an isosceles triangle. If the largest angle of the isosceles triangle is 92°, what is the measure of one of the equal angles?

20. Ashley designs a picture frame which is an equilateral triangle. Each side of the frame is 9 cm. She wants to put some ribbon to go around the frame for decoration. What is the length of ribbon needed?

21. Ben has a wooden triangular board shown on the right. He wants to paint the board. If the paint cost $0.7 per square meter, how much does he need to pay for the paint?

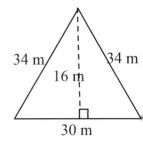

22. Henry cut out two triangles shown below. He thinks the triangle on the left is bigger. Is he correct?

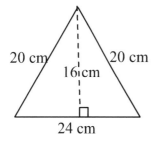

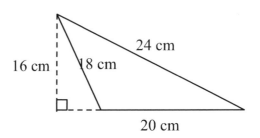

23. Dan has a sheet of paper shown on the right. If he cuts along the dotted line shown, he will have two right-angled triangles. The larger right-angled triangle is three times bigger than the smaller right-angled triangle. Find the value of a.

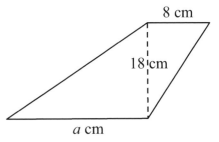

24. Jack has a square sheet of paper with each side of 20 cm. When he cuts along the diagonal of the square, he has two identical triangles. The total perimeters of the two triangles is 56 cm longer than the perimeter of the original square. What is the perimeter of one triangle?

Squares and Rectangles

What makes a shape a square or a rectangle?

Section Objectives

- Able to identify the characteristics of squares and rectangles
- Able to find the areas and perimeters of rectangles and square
- Know how to solve problem involving areas and perimeters of squares or rectangles

Key Study Points

Rectangles are four sided shapes with two pairs of equal sides and four right angles.

Square can be considered a special type of rectangle as it has all the properties of rectangles except that all four sides of a square are equal whereas in a rectangle, only opposite sides are equal.

These are the properties of rectangles and squares.

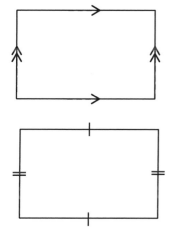
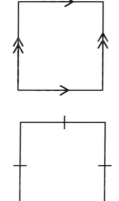

Opposite sides are parallel.

Opposite sides are equal.

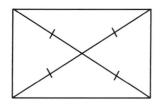 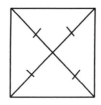 Diagonals are of the same length and bisect each other.

The perimeter of square = 4 × side length

The perimeter of rectangle = 2 × (width + length)

The area of square = side length × side length

The area of rectangle = width × length

Worked Examples

Example 1: Find the area and the perimeter of a square with the side length of 6 cm.

Area = 6 cm × 6 cm = 36 cm^2

Perimeter = 6 cm × 4 = 24 cm

A common mistake is mixing up 6 × 6 and 6 + 6 when looking for area. Also, remember to consider all four sides of the perimeter rather than just 2.

Example 2: The area of a rectangle is 35 m^2. If its length is 7 m, what is its width?

Area = width × length

35 = width × 7

Width = 5 m

Practice Questions

For questions 1 to 6, find the perimeter and the area of the shapes.

1.

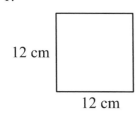

12 cm

12 cm

2.

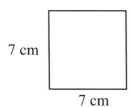

7 cm

7 cm

3.

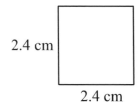

2.4 cm

2.4 cm

4.

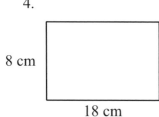

8 cm

18 cm

5.

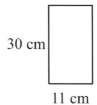

30 cm

11 cm

6.

19 cm

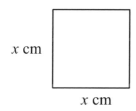

5 cm

For questions 7 to 15, find the unknowns.

7. Area = 225 cm^2

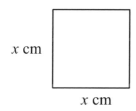

x cm

x cm

8. Perimeter = 84 cm

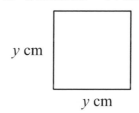

y cm

y cm

9. Area = 63 cm^2

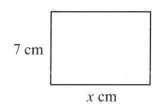

7 cm

x cm

10. Area = 184 cm^2

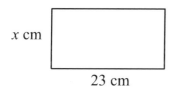

x cm

23 cm

11. Area = 64.8 cm^2

5.4 cm

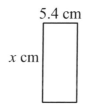

x cm

12. Perimeter = 120 cm

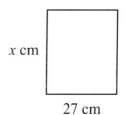

x cm

27 cm

13. Perimeter = 88 cm   14. Perimeter = 70 cm   15. Perimeter = 114 cm

13 cm [rectangle, x cm]   2x cm [rectangle, $5x$ cm] $3y + 1$ cm [rectangle]

y cm

16. The width of the classroom is 8 meters and the length is 22 meters. If the cost of carpet is $4.6 per meter, how much does it cost to replace the carpet?

17. Sam cuts out a square with the side length of 11 cm from a construction paper of the dimension 15 cm by 25 cm. What is the area of the construction paper left?

18. A square mirror has the side length of 34 cm. Frank is trying to wrap some tape around the mirror to protect the edge of the mirror. What is the length of tape needed?

19. A rectangular flowerbed is in the middle of a park. A 3-meter wide path surrounds the flower bed. If the dimension of the flowerbed is 35 meters by 55 meters, what is the area of the path?

20. Ben had a rectangular cardboard with the width of 23 cm. If he cut it in half along its length, he will have two identical squares.

(a) What is the area of the cardboard before it is cut in half?

(b) What is the total perimeter after the cardboard is cut in half?

Other Quadrilaterals

 What is the difference between a kite and a rhombus?

Section Objectives

- Know the characteristics of different quadrilaterals
- Able to identify different types of quadrilaterals using their characteristics
- Able to find the areas and perimeters of different quadrilaterals
- Know how to solve problem involving areas and perimeters of squares or rectangles

Key Study Points

Quadrilaterals are four sided shapes.

The interior angles of a quadrilateral sum up to 360 degrees.

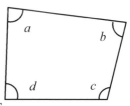

Other than rectangle and square, these are different types of quadrilaterals.

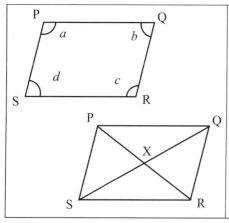

	Parallelogram
	Definition:
	Opposite sides are parallel. (PQ//SR, PS//QR)
	Properties:
	Opposite sides are equal. (PQ = SR, PS = QR)
	Opposite angles are equal. ($a = c$, $b = d$)
	Diagonals bisect each other. (PX = XR, SX = XQ)

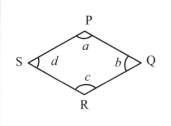 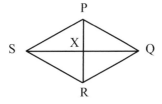	**Rhombus** Definition: All sides are equal. (PQ = QR = RS = SP) Properties: Opposite sides are parallel. (PQ//SR, SP//RQ) Opposite angles are equal. ($a = c$, $b = d$) Diagonals are perpendicular to each other. (PR⊥SQ) Diagonals bisect each other. (PX = XR, SX = XQ)
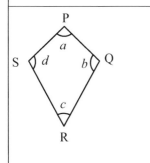	**Kite** Definition: Two pair of adjacent sides are equal. (SP = PQ, QR = SR) Properties: Opposite angles are equal. ($a = c$, $b = d$) Diagonals are perpendicular to each other. (PR⊥SQ)
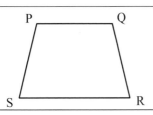	**Trapezium** Definition: One pair of opposite sides are parallel. (PQ//SR)

Perimeter of any quadrilateral is the sum of all four sides.

Areas for different quadrilaterals are calculated using formulas listed below.

The area of parallelogram = height × width

The area of trapezium = $\frac{1}{2}$ × (top + base) × height

Worked Examples

Example 1: Identify the following shapes and find the area.

(a)

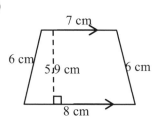

(b)

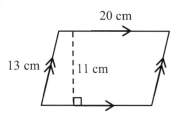

(a) A pair of opposite sides are parallel. This is a trapezium.

The area $= \frac{1}{2} \times (7 + 8) \times 5.9 = 44.25$ cm^2

(b) The opposite sides are parallel. This is a parallelogram.

The area $= 20 \times 11 = 220$ cm^2

Practice Questions

For questions 1 to 6, identify the following shapes.

1.

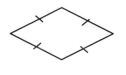

2.

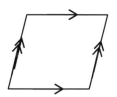

3.

4.

5.

6.

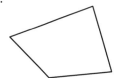

For questions 7 to 10, find the area of these shapes.

7.

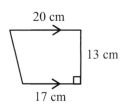

20 cm

13 cm

17 cm

8.

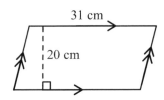

31 cm

20 cm

9.

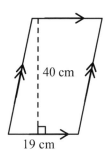

40 cm

19 cm

10.

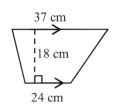

37 cm

18 cm

24 cm

For questions 11 to 15, find the unknowns.

11.

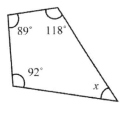

89°   118°

92°

x

12.

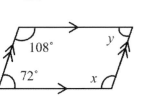

108°   y

72°   x

13.

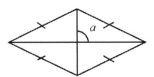

a

14.

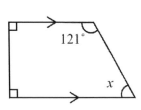

121°

x

15.

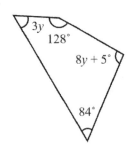

3y
128°

8y + 5°

84°

16. Sam has a piece of paper in the shape of an equilateral triangle. Sam cut along a straight line at the top of the equilateral triangle. If the part he cut out is also an equilateral triangle, what is the shape of the paper left?

17. In the figure, ABCD is a square. AF = AE. E and F is the midpoint of BC and DC.

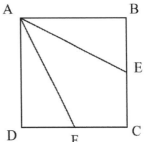

   (a) Identify the shape of AECF.
   (b) If ∠DAF = ∠FAE = ∠EAB, find the measure of ∠AFC.

3D Shapes

 What is the difference between a circle and a sphere?

Section Objectives

- Able to identify common 3D shapes and their nets
- Understand the basic terms for 3D shapes like "vertices", "edges" and "faces"

Key Study Points

2D shapes are flat and 3D shapes are not.

2D shapes have 2 dimensions: length and width.

3D shapes have 3 dimensions: length, width and height.

Some 3D shapes have same cross section along a length of the shapes and these 3D shapes are called prisms.

Most 3D shapes are made up of faces, edges and vertices.

Faces are surfaces. Edges are the lines where faces meet. Vertices are the corners.

Here are the common 3D shapes.

Name	Uniform cross section	Faces	Edges	Vertices
Cube	Square	6	12	8

Cuboid/Rectangular prism	Square or rectangle	6	12	8
Triangular prism	Triangle	5	9	6
Triangular-based pyramid /Tetrahedron	None	4	6	4
Square-based pyramid	None	5	8	5
Cylinder	Circle	3	2	1
Cone	None	2	1	1
Sphere	None	1	0	0

To find the volume of rectangular prism, we make use of the formula.

Volume = width × length × height

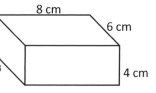

So, the volume of the prism on the right is 8 cm × 6 cm × 4 cm = 192 cm^3

Worked Example

Jack has some candles in the shape of a cube with edge of 4 cm. How many candles can he fit in the box shown on the left?

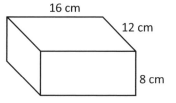

We can use division to find out how many candles can be along the length, width and height.

16 cm ÷ 4 cm = 4 candles

12 cm ÷ 4 cm = 3 candles

8 cm ÷ 4 cm = 2 candles

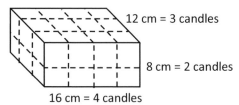

Therefore, the number of candles that can fit in the box is 4 × 3 × 2 = 24

Practice Questions

For questions 1 to 6, find the volume of these prisms.

1.

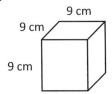

2.

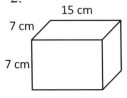

3.

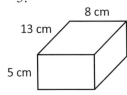

4.

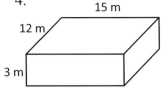

5.

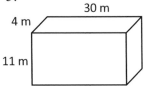

6.

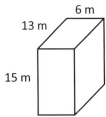

For questions 7 to 12, find the unknowns.

7. Volume = 90 cm^3

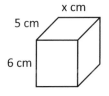

8. Volume = 88 cm^3

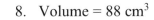

9. Volume = 243 cm^3

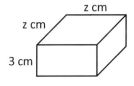

10. Volume = 98 m^3

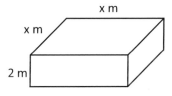

11. Volume = 256 m^3

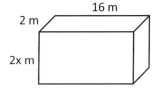

12. Volume = 144 m^3

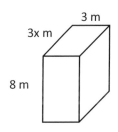

13. The base of a fish tank is 4 meters by 3 meters. If the water is filled up to the depth of 1.5 meters, what is the volume of the water in the fish tank?

14. A small juice box is 5 cm by 4 cm by 8 cm. A carton of milk is 6 cm by 8 cm by 12 cm. How much more volume does the carton of milk have?

15. A box with the dimension of 30 cm by 24 cm by 12 cm is filled completely with some wooden cubes with the edge of 3 cm. How many cubes are there?

16. An alarm clock is packed in a cubic box with the edge of 15 cm. The boxes are then packed into a bigger cubic box with the edge of 1.8 meters. How many alarm clocks can be fit in the bigger box?

Coordinates

How can I find a point on a grid?

Section Objectives

- Understand how to use coordinates to determine the location of points
- Know how to find the coordinates of vertices of rectangles and squares with information given

Key Study Points

Coordinates are the numbers that determine the position of a point on a graph or a grid. For example, the coordinates of point A are (3, 4). The first number is called the x-coordinate and the second number is called the y-coordinate. The coordinates of point B is (-4, 4) and the coordinates of point C is (3, -3).

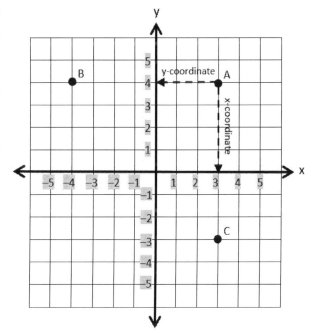

Points with same x-coordinates can be joined with a vertical line and the points with same y-coordinates can be joined with a horizontal line. We can join points A and C with a vertical line. Similarly, points A and B can be joined with a horizontal line.

The intersection of the two axes is called origin. The coordinates of origin are (0, 0). Any points to the right of the origin have positive x-coordinates. Any points above origin have positive y-coordinates.

All the points on the y-axis have 0 for their x-coordinates.

All the points on the x-axis have 0 for their y-coordinates.

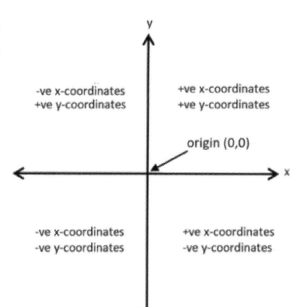

Worked Examples

Example 1: Which of the following can be the coordinates for points X and Y?

A. X (4, -4) Y (4, -4)

B. X (4, -4) Y (-4, 4)

C. X (-4, 4) Y (4, 4)

D. X (-4, 4) Y (4, -4)

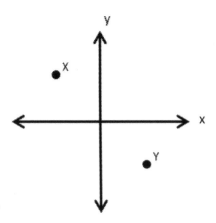

Point X is to the left of the origin => x-coordinate of point X is negative.

Point X is above the origin => y-coordinate of point X is positive.

Point Y is to the right of the origin => x-coordinate of point Y is positive.

Point Y is below the origin => y-coordinate of point X is negative.

Therefore, D is the answer.

Example 2: Line PQ is a horizontal line. Points P and Q are both x units away from the y axis. If the coordinates of Q are (7, 2), what are the coordinates of P?

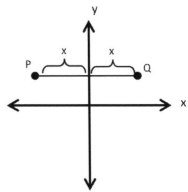

Since PQ is on the same horizontal line, they have the same y-coordinates. As the x-coordinate of point Q is 7, point Q is 7 units away from the y-axis. As a result, we can deduce that Point P is 7 units to the left of the y-axis. The x-coordinate is negative when it is to the left of the y

So, the coordinates of P are (-7, 2).

Example 3:   A(1, 8) and B (-3, -6) are the two opposite vertices of a rectangle. What are the coordinates of the other two vertices?

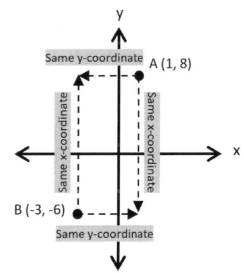

First, plot the two points on the grid.

Since the top left vertex is on the same horizontal line with point A, the y-coordinate of top left vertex is the same as point A. It is also on the same vertical line with point B and the x-coordinate of the top left vertex is the same as point B. So, the coordinates for the top left vertex are (-3, 8).

The bottom right vertex is on the same vertical line with point A. Therefore, the x-coordinate of bottom right vertex is the same as point A. It is also on the same horizontal line with point B and the y-coordinate of the bottom right vertex is the same as point B. So the coordinates for the bottom right vertex are (1, -6).

Practice Questions

1. Write the coordinates of the points on the grid.

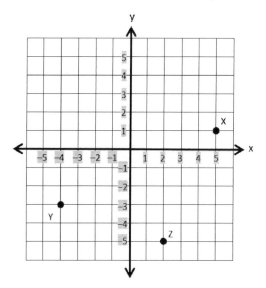

2. Which of the following can be the coordinates of points P and Q?

   A. P (-3, -3) Q (3, -3)

   B. P (-3, 3) Q (-3, -3)

   C. P (3, 3) Q (-3, 3)

   D. P (-3, 3) Q (3, 3)

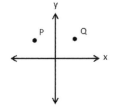

3. Which of the following can be the coordinates of points P and Q?

   A. P (-1, -3) Q (3, -1)

   B. P (2, -3) Q (1, -3)

   C. P (1, -3) Q (3, -2)

   D. P (3, -1) Q (2, -3)

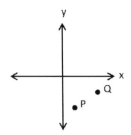

4. Which of the following point is on the x-axis?

   A. (0, -5)

   B. (3, 0)

C. (2, 8)

D. (9, 9)

5. Which of the following point is not on the y-axis?

A. (9, 0)

B. (0, -4)

C. (0, 0)

D. (0, 8)

6. A (1, -5) and B (-4, 7) are the two opposite vertices of a rectangle. What are the coordinates of the other two vertices?

7. A (3, 9) and B (-3, -1) are the two opposite vertices of a rectangle. What are the coordinates of the other two vertices?

8. A (-4, 9) and B (-7, 3) are the two opposite vertices of a rectangle. What are the coordinates of the other two vertices?

9. The four vertices of a square are located at (4, 6), (4, -7), (1, -7) and (1, 6). Which of the following points is inside the square?

A. (7, 5)

B. (-3, 1)

C. (3, -4)

D. (-6, 2)

10. The four vertices of a square are located at (-9, -3), (5, -3), (5, -9) and (-9, -9). Which of the following points is not inside the square?

A. (-4, -1)

B. (-6, -6)

C. (-2, -4)

D. (-5, -7)

Data Organization

 What is data? Why do we need to organize data?

Section Objectives

- Understand the importance of organizing data
- Know how to organize data using tables
- Know how to find information from a table

Key Study Points

Data is information.

Raw data is information as it is collected, without any processing. With raw data, it is difficult to draw conclusions or make interpretations. Therefore, it is important to organize data. Putting the raw data in a table is the most common way to organize data.

For example, the test scores of a group of students is an example of data.

Raw data – Students' Grades
B C A E D A A B C A
D A B B C A A A B B

Organized data

Grade	Frequency
A	8
B	6
C	3
D	2
E	1

In a table, data is organized in the column and rows. Related data can be found in the same column or row. **Frequency indicates the number of times a specific data occurs**.

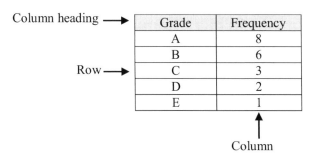

Grade	Frequency
A	8
B	6
C	3
D	2
E	1

Column heading → (points to top row)

Row → (points to Grade C row)

Column ↑

Continuous data (such as time or length) is grouped in ranges. It is important to remember that each range must have the same width for every group.

Height (cm)	Frequency
101 – 120	8
121 – 140	6
141 – 160	3
181 – 200	2
201 – 200	1

Another common way of organizing data is a two-way table. It is used when the data can belong two categories. Two-way table can show the relationship between the categories.

For example, this two-way table shows the relationship between the grade and gender of some students.

Number of grade 1 boys

	Boys	Girls	Total
Grade 1	9	11	20
Grade 2	15	10	25
Total	24	21	45

Total number of grade 1 students

Total number of girls

When the data is organized, we can use different diagrams or graph to present the data (which will be discussed in the next few sections).

Worked Examples

Example 1: With the given two-way table, find

Favorite Ice-cream Flavor

	Vanilla	Chocolate	Strawberry	Total
Adults	40			65
Children		45		80
Total	53	56	36	145

(a) the number of adults that like vanilla ice-cream the most.

We can go to the column under Vanilla and the row of adults to find the number of adults who like vanilla ice-cream the most. There are 40 adults that like vanilla ice-cream.

(a) the number of children that like strawberry ice-cream the most.

As the box with number of children that like strawberry ice-cream the most is empty, we need to work out the numbers. Making use of the numbers in other boxes can help us deduce the empty boxes.

	Vanilla	Chocolate	Strawberry	Total
Adults	40			65
Children	① $53 - 40 =$ 13	45	② $80 - 13 - 45 =$ 22	80
Total	53	56	36	145

① There are total of 53 people who chose Vanilla and 40 of them are adults. We can find out that there are 13 children who chose vanilla.

② There are in total 80 children. 45 of them chose chocolate and 13 of them chose vanilla. We can find out there are 22 children that chose strawberry.

As a result, there are 22 children that like strawberry ice-cream the most.

Example 2: Answer the questions using of the table shown below.

Result of a 100 m race

Time (seconds)	Frequency
10.0 – 10.9	2
11.0 – 11.9	3
12.0 – 12.9	7
13.0 – 13.9	10
14.0 – 14.9	9

(a) How many athletes were there?

To find out the number of athletes that were competing, we can sum up all the frequencies.

Therefore, the number of athletes = 2 + 3 + 7 + 10 + 9 = 31

(b) What was the fastest possible time and the slowest possible time to finish the race?

The first range is 10.0 – 10.9 seconds so the fastest possible time used to finish the race is 10.0 seconds. The last range is 14.0 – 14.9 seconds so the slowest possible time to finish the race is 14.9 seconds.

(c) What is the range of time that most athletes finished the race?

The range of 13.0 – 13.9 seconds has the highest frequency. Most of the athletes finished the race within 13.0 seconds to 13.9 seconds.

Practice Questions

1. These are the numbers of books that a group of students read in February.

   3 2 5 1 0 3 4 5 2 0 2 1 3 1 3 4 4 0 1 3

   (a) Fill in the missing details in the data table.

Number of books read	Frequency
0	
1	
2	
3	
4	
5	

(b) How many students are there in the group?

(c) How many students did not read any books in February?

2. These are the heights (measured in cm) of a class.

149 121 114 137 109 148 120 116 148 116

125 137 148 110 147 116 142 114 113 106

138 111 132 108 124

(a) Fill in the missing details in the data table.

Height (cm)	Frequency
101 – 110	
111 – 120	
121 – 130	

(b) How many students are there in the class?

(c) Which range of height has the most students?

3. This two-way table shows how a group of students travel to school and the distance they live from the school.

	Walk	School Bus	Total
Within 2 km	24	14	38
More than 2 km	11	36	47
Total	35	50	85

(a) How many students are there in total?

(b) How many students live more than 2 km away from the school?

(c) How many students live within 2 km from the school and take the school bus?

4. This two-way table shows the weather in the month of March and April.

	March	April	Total
Rain	4		
No Rain		12	
Total	31	30	61

(a) How many rainy days were there in total for the two months?

(b) Which month has more rainy days?

5. This two-way table shows the color of eyes and color of hair of a group of adults.

	Brown eyes	Blue eyes	Green eyes	Total
Black hair	21		18	50
Blond hair		27	21	
Brown hair	14			
Total	38	58		141

(a) How many adults are there in total?

(b) How many adults have green eyes?

(c) How many adults have blond hair?

(d) How many adults have brown hair and green eyes?

Pictograms, Bar Charts and Line Graphs

 How can we present data to help others understand it quickly?

Section Objectives

- Understand how to interpret pictograms, bar charts and line graphs
- Know how to create pictograms, bar charts and line graphs
- Know to distinguish between pictograms, bar charts or line graphs

Key Study Points

Pictograms, bar charts and line graphs are different ways of presenting data visually.

Pictograms present data with images. Since each image represents a chunk of data, some pictograms cannot be very accurate and precise.

Here is an example of a pictogram.

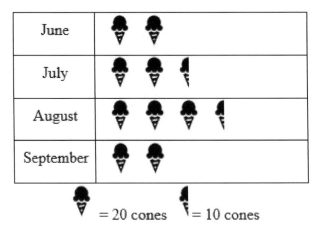

Bar graphs present data with bars and it is more accurate and precise than pictograms.

The bars can be vertical or horizontal. The following is an example of a bar graph with vertical bars.

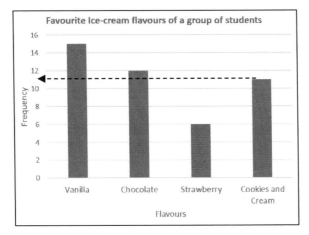

match the top of the bars to the markings on the axis to find the value the bar is representing

With pictograms and bar graphs, it is easier to compare the differences between the frequencies of different data.

To find out the trend of the data, we use line graphs.

This is an example of a line graph.

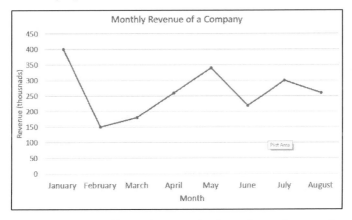

Making use of line graph we can easily make conclusion about the trend and see that there is a big decrease in the monthly revenue from January to February.

Sometimes, there is more than one set of data in a line graph. When reading line graphs with two sets of data, it is important to check the legends. This is an example of line graphs with two sets of data.

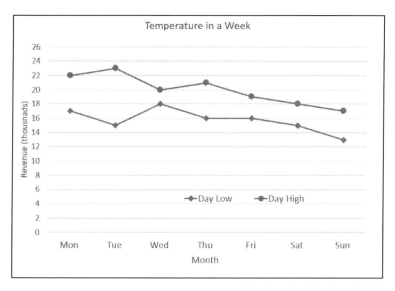

Temperature in a Week

Worked Examples

Example 1: Answer the questions according to the given pictogram.

Sales of donuts

Monday	
Tuesday	
Wednesday	
Thursday	
Friday	
Saturday	
Sunday	

= 40 donuts   = 20 donuts   = 10 donuts

(a) How many donuts were sold on Tuesday?

Each donut image represents 40 donuts and half donut represents 20 donuts

$40 + 40 + 20 = 100$

100 donuts are sold on Tuesday.

(b) On which day did the shop made the most sales?

On Saturday, the shop made the most sales.

(c) Compared to Sunday, how many more donuts were sold on Saturday?

180 donuts (4 × 40 + 20) were sold on Saturday and 130 donuts (3 × 40 + 10) were sold on Sunday.

Compared to Sunday, 50 more donuts were sold on Saturday.

Example 2: Create a bar chart based on the data table given on the money raised at a charity events by four people.

Name	Money raised ($)
Daniel	23
Ashley	17
Charles	19
Ben	10

Step 1: Prepare the axes and chart title.

We can get an idea of the chart title from the given information in the question. Also, it is a good idea to make use of the column heading of the given data table for the labels of the axes. It is important to make sure the scale of the axis cover the range of the data (in this case $10 to $23).

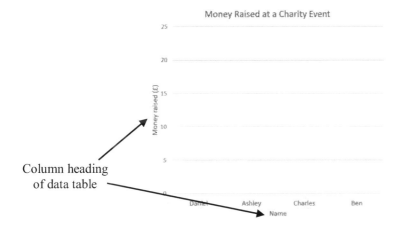

Column heading of data table

Step 2: Draw bars

Pay attention to the axis and the height/length of the bars.

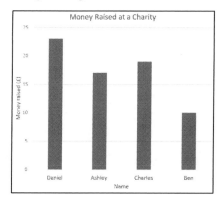

Example 3: This data table shows Emily's expenditure for the past week. Create a line graph based on the data table.

Name	Money Spent ($)
Mon	4
Tue	2
Wed	6
Thu	5
Fri	10
Sat	12
Sun	9

Step 1: Prepare the axes and chart title.

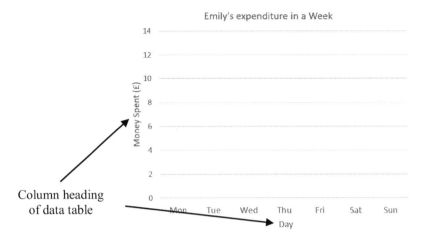

Column heading
of data table

Step 2: Plot the points according to the data table.

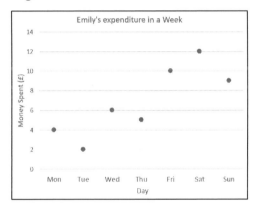

Step 3: link the points together with straight line.

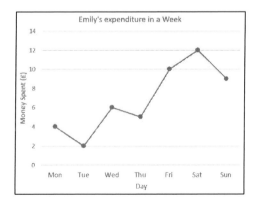

Practice Questions

1. This pictogram shows the number of Christmas cards that some children received this Christmas.

Name	Cards received
Sophia	✉✉✉✉
Paul	✉✉✉
Harry	✉✉✉⊠
Kathy	✉✉✉✉✉⊠
Olivia	✉✉⊠

✉ = 2 cards ⊠ = 1 card

(a) Who received the most number of cards?

(b) How many cards did Harry and Sophia receive in total?

(c) Compared to Paul, how many more cards did Kathy received?

2. This bar graph shows the grades of a class.

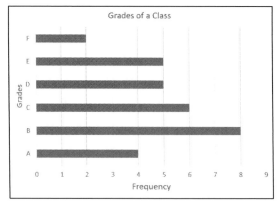

(a) How many students are there in the class?

(b) What is the grade attained by most students?

(c) How many students failed?

3. This bar graph shows the time a group of students spent reading in a week.

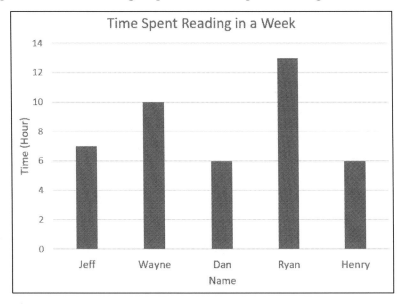

(a) How many students are there in the group?

(b) Who spent the most time reading in a week?

(c) Which two students spent the same time reading in a week?

4. A group of students answered a survey about how many pets they have at home. The results are organized in the data table below. Create a bar graph based on the data.

Number of pets	Number of students
No Pets	6
1 Pet	13
2 Pets	11
3 Pets	3
4 Pets	4
More than 4 pets	2

5. This line graph shows the forest coverage (measured in square kilometers) of a town.

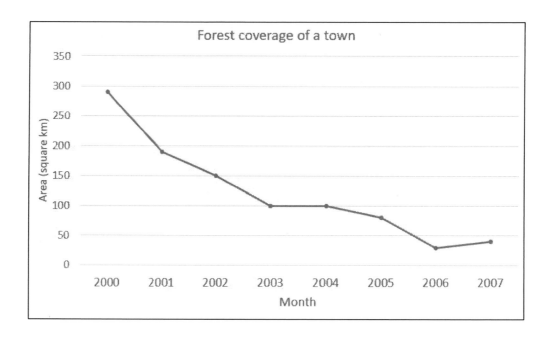

(a) Between which two years does the forest coverage stay the same?

(b) In which year does the forest coverage is the lowest?

(c) Between which two years does the forest coverage has the greatest decrease?

(d) What can we conclude about the general trend of the forest coverage of this town?

6. This line graph shows the highest and the lowest temperature of each day in a week.

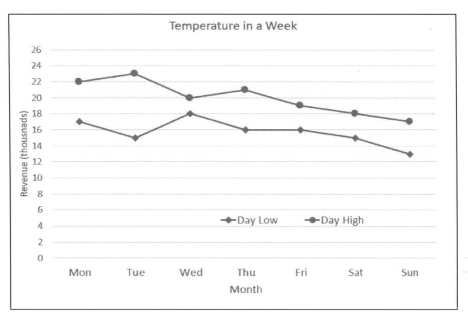

(a) Which day has the highest day low temperature?

(b) Which day has the lowest day high temperature?

(c) Which day has the smallest difference between the day high and day low?

7. This data table shows the number of absences in a class for the past week. Create a line graph based on the data table.

Day	Number of students
Mon	3
Tue	4
Wed	8
Thu	2
Fri	5

Pie Charts

 What is the difference between bar charts and pie charts?

Section Objectives

- Understand how to interpret pie charts
- Know how to create pie charts

Key Study Points

Pie charts is another way to present data by showing the proportion of data. It helps us compare the size of the data by the size of the sector in a circle.

The following pie chart shows the favorite pizza toppings of a group of people. Since the sector representing pepperoni is a half-circle, half of the group chose pepperoni as their favorite topping. Similarly, the quarter-circle representing pepper implies that quarter of the group chose pepper as their favorite topping.

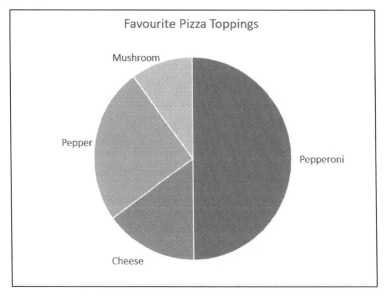

However, since we are not given the information of the number of people included in the survey, we do not know how many people chose each of the toppings.

Pie charts can show different information concerning the frequency of each data item, which can be any one (or more) of the following:

- the frequency of each data item
- percentage of each data item
- the degree of each sector

To create pie chart, it is important to remember to find the proportion of the frequency of each data item **out of the total frequency**. This proportion can then be turned into the degrees of the pie chart circle.

Here are the steps to create a pie chart based on a given data table shown here.

Favorite pet

Pet	Frequency
Dog	10
Cat	8
Fish	4
Rabbit	2

Step 1: Find the proportion of each item out of the total frequency.

Total frequency = 10 + 8 + 4 + 2 = 24

Then, we can find the proportion (in terms of fraction) for each item.

Pet	Frequency	Proportion
Dog	10	$\dfrac{10}{24} = \dfrac{5}{12}$
Cat	8	$\dfrac{8}{24} = \dfrac{1}{3}$

Fish	4	$\dfrac{4}{24} = \dfrac{1}{6}$
Rabbit	2	$\dfrac{2}{24} = \dfrac{1}{12}$

Step 2: Multiplying 360 degrees to each proportion to find the angle for each sector.

Pet	Frequency	Proportion	Degree
Dog	10	$\dfrac{10}{24} = \dfrac{5}{12}$	$\dfrac{5}{12} \times 360° = 150°$
Cat	8	$\dfrac{8}{24} = \dfrac{1}{3}$	$\dfrac{1}{3} \times 360° = 120°$
Fish	4	$\dfrac{4}{24} = \dfrac{1}{6}$	$\dfrac{1}{6} \times 360° = 60°$
Rabbit	2	$\dfrac{2}{24} = \dfrac{1}{12}$	$\dfrac{1}{12} \times 360° = 30°$

Step 3: draw the sectors according to the degrees in the pie chart.

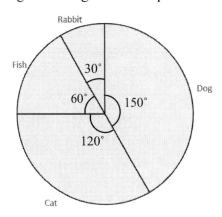

Step 4: Add appropriate title.

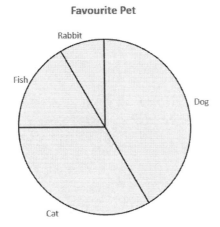

Worked Examples

Example 1: The pie chart shows the survey results of a group of students. Answer the questions based on the given pie chart.

(a) Which sports is most popular?
Since football has the highest percentage (32%), football is the most popular.

(b) If 50 students are surveyed, how many students chose baseball as their favorite sports?
50 × 16 % = 8

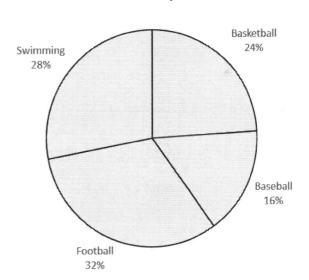

8 students chose baseball as their favorite sport.

Example 2: This pie chart shows the distribution of different positions of staff at an office.

Different positions of staff at an office

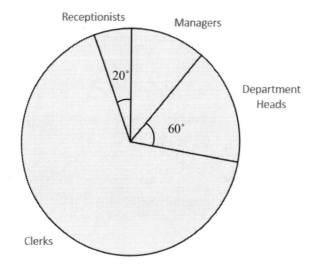

(a) There are 2 receptionists in the office. How many staff are there in total?

Since the angle of the sector represents the proportion of receptionist, we can find the total number of staff using division.

$2 \div \frac{20°}{360°} = 36$

There are 36 staff in the office.

(b) There are 4 managers in the office. How many clerks are there in total?

With 2 receptionists, the angle of the sector representing receptionists is 20°. As the number of managers is double the number of receptionists, the angle of the sector representing managers is also doubled the angle of the sector representing receptionist. The sector representing managers should be 40°.

The degrees around the circle is 360° and we can find the angle of the sector representing clerks = 360° − 20° − 40° − 60° = 240°.

The number of clerks in the office = $36 \times \frac{240°}{360°} = 24$

Practice Questions

1. This pie chart shows how Sean usually spend his day.

A Typical Day for Sean

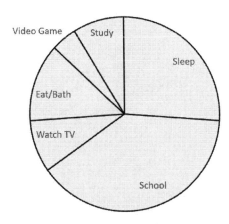

(a) What does Sean usually spend most of his time doing in a day?

(b) What does Sean usually spend the least amount of his time doing in a day?

(c) The sector representing sleep in the pie chart has an angle of 90°. How much time does he usually sleep?

2. This pie chart shows the distribution of Joe's salary.

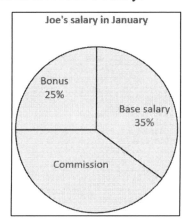

(a) If Joe's salary in January was $1000, what was his base salary in January?

(b) What made up most of Joe's salary in January?

3. This pie chart shows how a group of people go to work. Half of the people drive or take train to work.

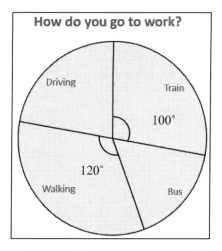

(a) There are 30 people walking to work. How many people are there in total?

(b) How many people take bus to work?

4. Noah counted the number of vehicles that pass by her house in an hour. Her findings are listed in the following data table. Create a pie chart based on the data table.

Vehicle Type	Frequency
Truck	4
Bus	8
Car	12

Venn Diagram

How can we present data that falls under different categories?

Section Objectives

- Understand the use of Venn diagram
- Able to solve problems with Venn diagram

Key Study Points

Venn diagram shows the relationship between different groups of things. Things that are enclosed in a circle are in the same group and things are in the overlapped area of the circle belong to both groups.

For example, this is a Venn diagram that shows the group of animals that can live in the water and/or on the land.

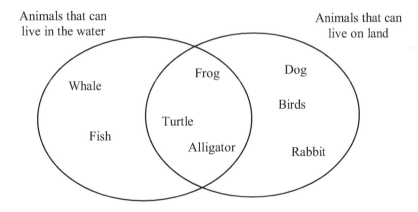

Sometimes, there are more than two groups. Grace made a Venn Diagram to group her friends that are in the same class with her.

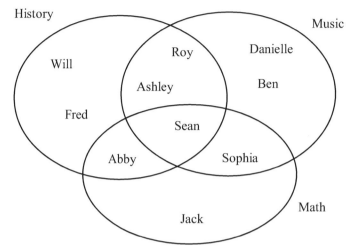

From the diagram, we can see four different overlapping areas. The overlapped area in the middle shows that Sean takes all three subjects. Similarly, Roy and Ashley take history and music.

Instead of listing the things (or people) in a group, the number of things (or people) will be shown in some Venn diagrams. The Venn diagram below shows that 9 people have only dogs as pets and 8 people have only cats as pets. The overlap area shows that 4 people have both dogs and cats as pets.

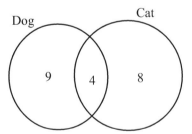

It is important to remember that there are 12 people that have cats (not only cats) because the total number that is enclosed in the circle of cats is 4+8 = 12 instead of just 8!

Also, if a number is <u>outside of all the circles</u> in the Venn diagram, the number represents the people surveyed who <u>do not belong to any group</u>.

Worked Examples

Example 1: This Venn diagram shows the allergy situation in a class.

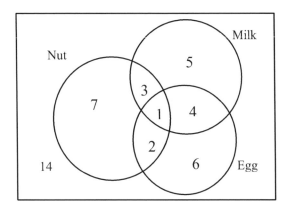

(a) How many students has no allergy?

14 students have no allergy.

(b) How many students are only allergic to egg?

6 students are only allergic to egg.

(c) How many students has two kinds of allergy?

The shaded areas are areas with two
overlapping circles which means the
students have two kinds of allergy.

3 + 4 + 2 = 9

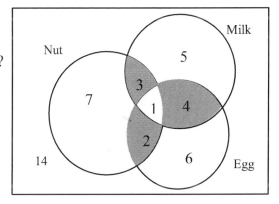

(d) How many students have milk allergy?

The shaded areas represents all students who have milk allergy.

The number of students with milk allergy

= 5 + 3 + 1 + 4

= 13

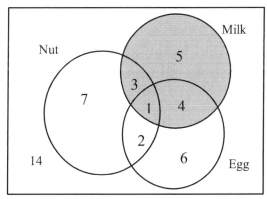

Example 2: Based on the given information, complete the Venn diagram with appropriate numbers.

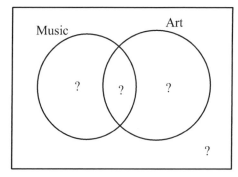

A group of 20 students were asked whether they like Music or Art or both.

3 students said they like neither. 8 students said they only like Music and 4 said they like both Music and Art.

Step 1: Fill out the given numbers to the appropriate area.

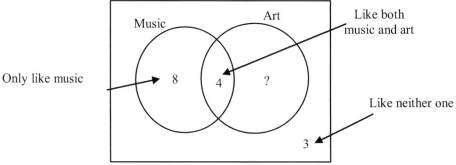

Step 2: find the numbers in the area that are still unknown

Since 20 students were surveyed, the number of students that only like art is

$20 - 8 - 4 - 3 = 5$

Therefore, the completed Venn diagram should look like the one on the right.

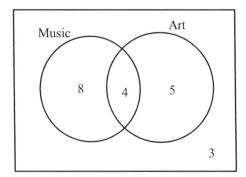

Practice Questions

1. This Venn diagram shows the flavor of ice-cream that a group of friends ordered at the ice-cream shop.

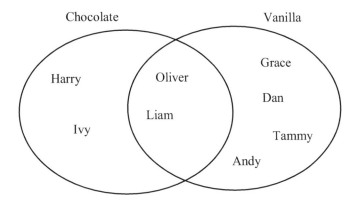

   (e) Which flavor did Ivy order?

   (f) How many flavors did Liam order?

   (g) How many people ordered only vanilla flavor?

   (h) How many people ordered two flavors?

2. This Venn diagram shows the number of nurses that might work at the day shift or night shift.

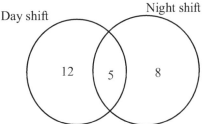

   (a) How many nurses might work both shifts?

   (b) How many nurses might only work during the day?

   (c) How many nurses are there in total?

3. This Venn diagram shows the languages that a group of students can speak.

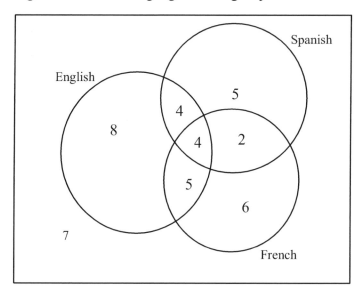

(a) How many students can only speak Spanish?

(b) How many students can speak three languages?

(c) How many students can speak only two languages?

(d) How many students can speak Spanish and French?

4. This Venn diagram shows the electronic devices that a group of students have.

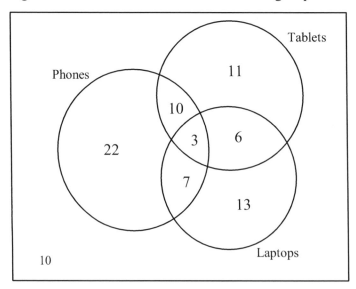

(a) How many students have phones?

(b) How many students have phones and tablets?

(c) Are there more students that have tablets or laptops?

5. Based on the given information, complete the Venn diagram with appropriate numbers.

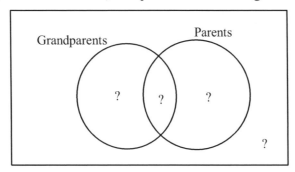

A group of 28 adults were asked who they lived with.

18 said they live on their own. 3 adults live with only their parents and 2 adults live with both their parents and grandparents.

6. Based on the given information, complete the Venn diagram with appropriate numbers.

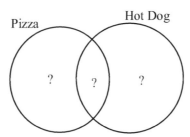

A group of 16 children were at a birthday party.

8 children had hot dog and 12 children had pizza.

Mean, Mode and Median

 How can we know which class performed better in a test?

Section Objectives

- Understand the definitions of mean, mode and median
- Able to compute the mean, mode and median of a set of data
- Know how to compare two sets of data using their means

Key Study Points

Mean is also called average. The mean of a set of data can be found by summing up all the data and dividing by the number of data points.

For example,

Data set: 9, 7, 5, 8, 3

The mean of the above data set $= \frac{9+7+5+8+3}{5} = 6.4$

Mean is one way to find the center where the data is distributed. It is also a way to compare different sets of data.

For example, these are the scores that two classes have for a math test.

Scores of students in Mr. Smith's Class: 15, 18, 16, 20, 11, 15, 12, 10, 13, 12

Scores of students in Mr. John's Class: 20, 20, 10, 18, 12, 16, 17, 11, 20, 10

The mean of math test scores in Mr. Smith's class $= \frac{15+18+16+20+11+15+12+10+13+12}{10} = 14.2$

The mean of math test scores in Mr. John's class $= \frac{20+20+10+18+12+16+17+11+20+10}{10} = 15.4$

Since the average test scores in Mr. John's class is higher, his class is generally better in the test. Remember mean can only give us a way to represent the <u>distribution of the data</u>. In this case, we can find some students that have higher scores in Mr. Smith's class than in Mr. John's class but with the mean, we can conclude that the students in Mr. John's class are **<u>generally</u>** better.

Mode is another way of describing how the data is distributed.

Mode is the data that appears the maximum number of times in the data set.

For example, the mode for following data set is 4.

4, 4, 4, 5, 6, 7, 7, 8, 8, 9

Sometimes, there are two modes for a data set. The following data set has two modes: 13, 19.

2, 5, 7, 13, 13, 18, 19, 19, 21

Median refers to the value in the "middle" of the data set.

To find the median, we need to line up the data in ascending (or descending) order.

For example, a data set is given: 5, 8, 1, 4, 6, 9, 2

To find the median, we need to first arrange the numbers in order 1, 2, 4, 5, 6, 8, 9

Since there are 7 data points in this set, the middle value is the 4th value. The median of this data set is 5.

In a data set with even number of data, the median will be the average of the two numbers in the middle.

For example, there are even number of data in this set: 5, 11, 18, 19, 20, 22.

The median will be the average of the two numbers, which are the 3rd and 4th numbers. Therefore, the median for this data set is the average of 18 and 19, which is 18.5.

Worked Examples

Example 1: If the mean of the data set below is 6, find the unknown value.

5, 1, 6, 8, x, 9

We can find the unknown by putting them into the formula we used to find the mean.

$$\frac{5 + 1 + 6 + 8 + x + 9}{6} = 6$$

$$5 + 1 + 6 + 8 + x + 9 = 36$$

$$x + 29 = 36$$

$$x = 7$$

Practice Questions

For questions 1 to 6, find the mean, median and mode of the data set.

1. 4, 6, 9, 7, 9

2. 18, 29, 24, 55, 24

3. 51, 32, 57, 89, 64, 32, 40, 41

4. 25, 39, 16, 16, 45, 89, 45, 76

5. 43, 2, 10, 41, 55, 41, 22, 22, 65, 22

6. 121, 158, 44, 72, 95, 102, 184, 72, 102, 98

For questions 7 to 10, find the unknowns.

7. Mean = 4

   Data set = 8, 1, 5, x, 3

8. Mean = 7.8

   Data set = 9, 6, 2, x, 7

9. Mean = 31

   Data set = 24, 39, 25, 44, x, 37, 29, 41, 50, 14

10. Mean = 7.4

    Data set = 9, 12, 8.4, 7.6, x, 5.5, 6.9, 7.6

11. A data set is given: 6, 9, 11, 15, 19. If the following number is added to the set, is the median going to be greater, smaller or remain unchanged?

(a) 2

(b) 11

(c) 21

12. A data set is given: 22, 16, 31, 52, 44, 33. If the following number is added to the set, is the median going to be greater, smaller or remain unchanged?

(a) 31

(b) 37

(c) 39

13. A data set is given: 94, 135, 156, 135, 191, 117. If 135 is added to the set, which of the following will be changed?

A. Mean   C. Median

B. Mode   D. All three will remain unchanged

14. A data set is given: 17, 15, 6, 9, 11, 14, 19, 21, 14. If 15 is added to the set, which of the following will remain unchanged?

A. Mean   C. Median

B. Mode   D. All three will be changed

15. Ben is 15 years old. He has 3 younger brothers which are 4 years old, 7 years old and 11 years old. What is the average age of the four brothers?

16. These are the heights (measured in cm) of two classes.

Ms. Ashley's class: 124, 145, 122, 114, 138, 129, 119, 140, 125, 137

Ms. Jenny's class: 113, 127, 115, 129, 118, 141, 132, 153, 110, 116

(a) Find the mean height of the two classes.

(b) What can you conclude from the mean height?

17. An athlete is practicing a 100-meter race. These are his times (measured seconds) of finishing 100 meters during the two phases of his training.

First phase: 13.4, 14.5, 14.1, 13.2, 14.7, 15.2, 14.9, 14.6, 13.6, 14.2, 13.9, 14.7

Second phase: 11.9, 12.3, 12.7, 12.1, 13.5, 12.4, 12.8, 12.3, 12.0, 16.1, 11.8, 11.9

(a) Find the mean time to finish running 100 meters during the two phases.

(b) What can the coach conclude from these two phases of training?

18. The following table shows the average rainfall of six months.

Month	Rainfall (mm)
January	21.5
February	11.5
March	18
April	10
May	17.6
June	40

(a) What is the average rainfall of first three months of this year?

(b) Joe thinks there is generally more rain in March than February. Is he correct? Explain.

(c) Is it possible to find a day in April with more than 10 mm of rain? Explain.

PROBABILITY

Introduction to Probability

 What is the likelihood of rolling an even number using a standard dice?

Section Objectives

- Understand what probability is
- Able to find probability of simple events
- Know how to compare probabilities of different events

Key Study Points

Probability is the likelihood of an event happening. Probability is a value between 0 and 1 and can be in the form of decimal or fraction.

Probability of 1 means an event will definitely happen and probability of 0 means an event will definitely not happen. The closer the probability is to 1, the higher the chance of that event happening and vice versa.

The probability of an event happening is defined by $\dfrac{\text{favorable outcomes}}{\text{all possible outcomes}}$

For example, there are two equally likely outcomes of tossing a coin – head or tail. So, the probability of getting a tail is $\frac{1}{2}$ and the probability of getting a head is $\frac{1}{2}$. The probability of getting a tail and getting a head is the same.

Many probability questions make use of playing cards, so it is a good idea to know that there are 52 cards in a deck of playing cards. Among the 52 cards, there are 13 of each of the four suits (spades, hearts, clubs, diamonds). Each suit includes an ace, a king, a queen and a jack and numbers 2 to 10.

Worked Examples

Example 1: Find the probability of

(a) rolling a 4 with a standard dice

There are 6 possible outcomes; 1, 2, 3, 4, 5, 6.

There is only 1 favorable outcome, which is 4.

So, the probability of rolling a 4 is $\frac{1}{6}$

(b) rolling an even number with a standard dice

The number of possible outcomes of a standard dice are still 6.

There are 3 favorable outcomes and they are 2, 4 and 6.

So, the probability of rolling an even number is $\frac{3}{6} = \frac{1}{2}$.

(c) Which is more likely, rolling a 4 or rolling an even number?

The probability of rolling a 4 is $\frac{1}{6}$ and the probability of rolling an even number is $\frac{1}{2}$. Since $\frac{1}{2} > \frac{1}{6}$, rolling an even number is more likely than rolling a 4.

Practice Questions

1. There are 14 marbles in a bag. 5 of the marbles are green and 9 of the marbles are red. What is the probability of picking a green marble?

2. What is the probability of rolling a 3 with a standard dice?

3. There are three pairs of red socks and one pair of white socks in a drawer. If Hannah picked a pair of socks from the drawer, which color is more likely to be picked?

4. There are 7 blue balls and 3 red balls in a bag. What is the probability of picking a blue ball from the bag?

5. There are 6 cups of coffee, 4 cups of juice and 4 cups of water on the table. What is the probability of picking a cup of coffee?

6. The following are the shapes that Angela cut out.

   (a) If a shape is picked randomly, what is the probability of picking a diamond shape?

   (b) If a shape is picked randomly, what is the probability of picking a star shape?

   (c) Which shape is the most likely to be picked?

7. What is the probability of rolling the same number with two standard dice?

8. A standard stack of playing cards are shuffled and a card is picked randomly.

   (a) What is the probability of picking a card of diamond?

   (b) What is the probability of picking a King?

   (c) What is the probability of picking a red card?

   (d) Which is more likely, picking a Queen or picking a card of clubs?

Pre-test

1. 78

2. 86

3. 56

4. 7900

5. 25

6. 84

7. $\frac{5}{6}$

8. $\frac{31}{7}$

9. $\frac{11}{20}$

10. $\frac{3}{5}$

11. 170%, 0.9, $\frac{3}{4}$

12. $9\frac{3}{25}$

13. \$3,750

14. 3 : 4 : 4

15. 3 : 7

16. 700 ml

17. 6

18. $7 - a$

19. $- 4$

20. $- 4$

21. 21

22. 135 minutes

23. 10: 45 a.m.

24. \$2.60

25. 5600 g

26. 500 mm

27. 1.65 L

28. A

29. 63 cm^2

30. 6

31. C

32. B

33. $(- 4, - 2)$

34.

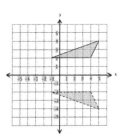

35. $(0, 5), (1, 6), (5, 1)$

36.

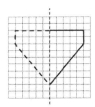

37. 4

38. Monday

39. Most people do not think the sales tax should be increased

40. 27

41. 14

42. $\frac{5}{14}$

Understanding Numbers

Place Values

1. 700,000

2. 20,000

3. Nine hundred seventy-eight thousand five hundred thirty-five

4. One million two hundred forty-one thousand eighty

5. 27,833,056

6. 1,704,067

7. $5 \times 10000000 + 0 \times 1000000 + 2 \times 100000 + 4 \times 10000 + 7 \times 1000 + 7 \times 100 + 7 \times 10 + 5$

8. $2 \times 10000 + 2 \times 1000 + 4 \times 100 + 9 \times 10 + 0$

Negative Numbers

1. $x = -46, y = -41$

2. $p = 0, q = 4$

3. B

4. C

5. -77, -55, 0, 14, 16, 66

6. -185, -85, -15, 15, 85

7. 99, 59, 39, -29, -49, -69

Decimal Numbers

1. 8 tenths

2. 4 thousandths

3. Thirty-four and seven tenths

4. One hundred twenty-seven and seventy-four thousandths

5. $2.9 = 2 \times 1 + 9 \times \frac{1}{10}$

6. $7.456 = 7 \times 1 + 4 \times \frac{1}{10} + 5 \times \frac{1}{100} + 6 \times \frac{1}{1000}$

7. $x = 0.33$ and $y = 0.36$

8. $m = -3.87$ and $n = -3.83$

9. $p = 7.28$ and $q = 7.3$

10. $a = -0.05$ and $b = 0.1$

11. 6.1, 6.15, 6.6, 6.65, 8.76, 8.8

12. 9.22, 9.2, 3.22, 3.2, 1.22, 1.2,

13. -5.42, -4.25, -2.45, 2.45, 4.25, 5.42

14. 17.35, 17.34, 17.3, -17.34, -17.345, -
    17.35

15. A

16. C

17. A

18. C

19. B

20. B

Rounding Off

1. 7100
2. 350
3. 116000
4. 9760000
5. 1.8
6. 31.32
7. 8.623
8. 3.0
9. 99.12

10. 53.500
11. (a) 30000
    (b) 31000
    (c) 31000
    (d) 31000
    (e) 31000
    (f) 31000.0
    (g) 31000.00
    (h) 30999.997

12. C
13. B
14. A
15. D
16. C
17. B
18. D
19. B
20. A

Estimation and Error

1. $19.9 \times 8.2 \approx 20 \times 8 = 160$
2. $31.1 \times 10.4 \approx 31 \times 10 = 310$
3. $79521 + 8.99 \approx 80000 + 9 = 80009$
4. $901105 + 157700 \approx 900000 + 160000 = 1060000$
5. $5.22301 - 0.1972 \approx 5 - 0.2 = 4.8$
6. $28993 - 8742 \approx 29000 - 9000 = 20000$
7. $82101 \div 9.5 \approx 82000 \div 10 = 8200$
8. $14070 \div 13.9975 \approx 14000 \div 14 = 1000$
9. (a) The mayor estimated the last year's population to 55000 and this year's population to 60000. Therefore, he estimated "an increase of 5000 in population".

(b) The actual population increase is 60128 – 54910 = 5218

The error in his estimation is 5218 – 5000 = 218

10. John's mom estimated that John will grow 5 cm every year. She then rounded John's current height to 105. Therefore, she estimated $105 + 5 \times 5 = 130$cm

11. (a) Ben estimated the dimension of the room to 5 meters by 9 meters. He also estimated the cost of the flooring is $10 per meter.

(b) Ben rounded down the size of the room and he also rounded down the cost of the flooring. So, his estimation will be less than the actual cost of the floorings.

Basic Arithmetic Operations

Four Arithmetic Operations with Whole Numbers

1. (a) Multiplication	8. 210	17. 35
(b) Addition	9. 1512	18. 15
(c) Division	10. 12441	19. 177
2. 11361	11. 175	20. 33
3. 1401	12. 21	21. 32
4. 22449	13. 379	22. 33
5. 153	14. 21 R3	23. 22
6. 2409	15. 30 R8	24. 94
7. 32095	16. 1973 R4	25. 99

Multiplying 10, 100 and 1000 and Dividing by 10, 100 and 1000

1. 60	8. 699	15. 0.34
2. 280	9. 86010	16. 6.43
3. 36	10. 975000	17. 0.61
4. 0.9	11. 2350000	18. 0.2
5. 700	12. 19755000	19. 6.54
6. 4100	13. 0.9	20. 0.054
7. 540	14. 70	21. 0.079

22. 4.387

23. 0.0035

24. 0.000986

25. (a) Correct
   (b) Incorrect
   (c) Correct

(d) Correct
(e) Incorrect
(f) Correct

Four Arithmetic Operations with Negative Numbers

1. 65.6
2. 48.797
3. 132.75
4. 5.288
5. 52.9
6. 392.41
7. 62.12

8. 34.28
9. 1.5
10. 7.049
11. 17.536
12. 7.87056
13. 12
14. 74

15. 46
16. 8.1
17. 7.4
18. 130
19. 500
20. 1780

Four Arithmetic Operations with Negative Numbers

1. −14
2. −18
3. 30
4. 9
5. −48
6. 8
7. 46
8. 24

9. −77
10. 155
11. −17
12. −9
13. 92
14. 25
15. 3
16. 85

17. 4.6
18. −6.34
19. −3.2
20. −2.352
21. 52.8
22. −59.59

Factors and Multiples

Factors, Multiples and Prime Numbers

1. 1, 2, 3, 6
2. 1, 5, 25
3. 1, 3, 7, 21
4. 1, 2, 3, 6, 9, 18

5. 1, 19
6. 1, 29
7. 1, 3, 13, 39

8. 1, 2, 4, 5, 10, 20, 25, 50, 100
9. 1, 17

17 is a prime number.

10. 1, 3, 9, 27.

27 is a composite number.

11. 3, 11

12. 2, 3, 7

13. 1×7

14. $2 \times 3 \times 5$

15. 2×2

16. $2 \times 2 \times 11$

17. $3 \times 5 \times 5$

18. $2 \times 2 \times 2$

19. $2 \times 2 \times 3 \times 3 \times 3$

20. $3 \times 3 \times 3 \times 5 \times 5$

21. 6, 12, 18, 24, 30

22. 4, 8, 12, 16, 20, 24, 28, 32

23. 7, 14, 21, 28, 35, 42

24. 80, 90, 100, 110, 120, 130, 140, 150

25. 204, 221, 238, 255, 272, 289

26. (a) False (b) True (c) True

(d) True because 38 is the multiples of 2 and 19, which both are prime numbers

(e) True, any number is its own multiple and factor. For example, 12 is its own factor as because $1 \times 12 = 12$. At the same time, 12 is its first multiple because $1 \times 12 = 12$.

(f) False, prime numbers are the numbers with only itself and 1 as its factors.

(g) True, prime number can be expressed in prime factorization too. Any prime number can be expressed as the product of 1 and itself.

LCM and GCD

1. GCD: 3 LCM: 30

2. GCD: 6 LCM: 36

3. GCD: 7 LCM: 147

4. GCD: 8 LCM: 120

5. GCD: 5 LCM: 385

6. GCD: 2 LCM: 176

7. GCD: 5 LCM: 900

8. GCD: 12 LCM: 360

9. GCD: 9 LCM: 540

10. GCD:5

LCM: 78000

Square and Cube Numbers

1. 64

2. 169

3. 36

4. 25

5. 8

6. 1331

7. −343

8. −512.

9. No

10. Yes

11. No

12. No

13. No

14. Yes

15. No

16. Yes

Fractions, Decimals and Percentages

Fraction and Equivalent Fraction

1. $\frac{1}{2}$

2. $\frac{1}{3}$

3. $\frac{3}{4}$

4. $\frac{2}{3}$

5. $\frac{2}{3}$

6. $\frac{2}{3}$

7. $\frac{27}{61}$

8. $\frac{16}{25}$

9. No

10. Yes

11. Yes

12. No

13. No

14. Yes

15. Yes

16. No

Mixed Numbers and Improper Fractions

1. Improper fraction

2. Mixed number

3. Improper fraction

4. Proper fraction

5. Proper fraction

6. Mixed number

7. $\frac{12}{5}$

8. $\frac{16}{9}$

9. $\frac{19}{5}$

10. $\frac{55}{7}$

11. $\frac{13}{4}$

12. $\frac{38}{7}$

13. $1\frac{1}{3}$

14. $2\frac{4}{5}$

15. $2\frac{5}{7}$

16. $3\frac{1}{11}$

17. $4\frac{5}{12}$

18. $3\frac{19}{24}$

Multiplying and Dividing Fractions

1. $\frac{8}{15}$

2. $\frac{16}{21}$

3. $\frac{9}{5}$

4. $\frac{9}{8}$

5. $\frac{20}{21}$

6. $\frac{16}{35}$

7. $\frac{9}{22}$

8. $\frac{12}{35}$

9. $\frac{24}{35}$

10. $\frac{160}{81}$

11. $\frac{14}{3}$

12. 10

13. $\frac{12}{7}$

14. $\frac{1}{15}$

15. $\frac{35}{12}$

16. $\frac{9}{25}$ 18. $\frac{6}{25}$ 20. $\frac{7}{81}$

17. $\frac{3}{5}$ 19. $\frac{3}{10}$

21. $\frac{3}{8} \times 6 = 2\frac{1}{4}$

He can read $2\frac{1}{4}$ books in 6 days.

22. $7\frac{3}{4} \times 5\frac{1}{3} = \frac{31}{4} \times \frac{16}{3} = \frac{124}{3} = 41\frac{1}{3}$

Nancy made $\$41\frac{1}{3}$ on Wednesday.

23. $15\frac{1}{2} \div 5 = \frac{31}{2} \times \frac{1}{5} = \frac{31}{10} = 3\frac{1}{10}$

Fred can spend $\$3\frac{1}{10}$ each day.

24. $27\frac{1}{2} \div 1\frac{1}{4} = 22$

Ben ran 22 days in March.

25. $9\frac{3}{8} \div 5 \div 2\frac{1}{2} = \frac{75}{8} \times \frac{1}{5} \times \frac{5}{2} = \frac{3}{4}$

Each tailor makes $\frac{3}{4}$ jacket in one hour.

$\frac{3}{4} \times 3\frac{1}{3} = 2\frac{1}{2}$

One tailor can make $2\frac{1}{2}$ jackets in $3\frac{1}{3}$ hours.

Comparing Fractions

1. $\frac{1}{7} < \frac{3}{7}$

2. $\frac{2}{5} < \frac{2}{3}$

3. $\frac{5}{9} < \frac{7}{12}$

4. $\frac{5}{9} < \frac{5}{7} < \frac{5}{6}$

5. $\frac{5}{12} < \frac{7}{15} < \frac{2}{3}$

6. $\frac{7}{18} < \frac{11}{24} < \frac{13}{16}$,

7. $\frac{3}{7} < 1\frac{1}{7} < \frac{9}{7}$

8. $\frac{11}{10} < 1\frac{1}{4} < \frac{11}{6}$

9. $\frac{41}{32} < 1\frac{17}{24} < 2\frac{1}{16}$

10. $\frac{7}{8} > \frac{1}{8}$

11. $\frac{2}{4} > \frac{2}{7}$

12. $\frac{8}{15} > \frac{5}{18}$

13. $\frac{3}{8} > \frac{3}{11} > \frac{3}{14}$

14. $\frac{5}{6} > \frac{11}{15} > \frac{4}{9}$

15. $\frac{10}{21} > \frac{11}{49} > \frac{5}{27}$

16. $1\frac{4}{5} > \frac{8}{5} > \frac{3}{5}$

17. $2\frac{5}{12} > \frac{7}{3} > \frac{22}{15}$

18. $\frac{63}{20} > 3\frac{1}{15} > 2\frac{17}{25}$

19. No, $2\frac{9}{10} < \frac{21}{5}$

20. First route is faster as $\frac{7}{12} < \frac{2}{3}$

21. He biked more as $7\frac{2}{3} > \frac{22}{3}$

22. No, $\frac{7}{10} > \frac{5}{9}$

Adding and Subtracting Fractions

1. $\frac{5}{9}$

2. $\frac{2}{3}$

3. $1\frac{4}{5}$

4. $3\frac{1}{2}$

5. $9\frac{1}{2}$

6. $\frac{3}{7}$

7. $\frac{3}{7}$

8. $1\frac{2}{3}$

9. $3\frac{2}{3}$

10. $1\frac{3}{5}$

11. $\frac{13}{15}$

12. $1\frac{3}{50}$

13. $1\frac{23}{36}$

14. $3\frac{37}{120}$

15. $6\frac{13}{48}$

16. $\frac{1}{10}$

17. $\frac{23}{42}$

18. $\frac{25}{108}$

19. $4\frac{19}{96}$

20. $2\frac{67}{90}$

21. $\frac{19}{48}$

22. $\frac{2}{3}$

23. $2\frac{83}{90}$

24. $6\frac{53}{70}$

Fractions, Decimals and Percentage

1. $0.55, \frac{11}{20}$

2. $0.89, \frac{89}{100}$

3. $0.243, \frac{243}{1000}$

4. $2.13, 2\frac{13}{100}$

5. $5.76, 5\frac{19}{25}$

6. $6.146, 6\frac{73}{500}$

7. $30\%, \frac{3}{10}$

8. $85\%, \frac{17}{20}$

9. $47.5\%, \frac{19}{40}$

10. $158\%, 1\frac{29}{50}$

11. $396\%, 3\frac{24}{25}$

12. $1557.4\%, 15\frac{287}{500}$

13. $0.7, 70\%$

14. $0.2, 20\%$

15. $0.75, 75\%$

16. $3.5, 350\%$

17. $4.1875, 418.75\%$

18. $3.875, 387.5\%$

19. $63\% > 0.5 > \frac{1}{8}$

20. $\frac{1}{4} > 0.24 > 2.4\%$

21. $0.35 > \frac{1}{3} > 30\%$

22. $6.9 > \frac{69}{100} > 6.9\%$

23. $5 > 50\% > \frac{1}{5}$

24. $9.2 > 900\% > \frac{9}{2}$

Percentage Problem

1. 3
2. 5
3. 32
4. 19.2
5. 20.68
6. 104.52
7. 403.1
8. 3937.6
9. 50%
10. 60%
11. 72%
12. 31.25%
13. 62.5%
14. 33%
15. 150%
16. 224%
17. 5 apples
18. 8 managers
19. 75%
20. 22.5%

21. $\frac{54}{26+54} = \frac{54}{80} = 67.5\%$

22. (a) 48 pounds (b) 30% (c) $(240 - 48 - 72) \times 45\% = 120 \times 45\% = 54$ pounds

23. (a) 50 dresses (b) 21% (c) $200 \times 24\% \times 25\% = 48 \times 25\% = 12$ jeans

Ratio and Proportion

Ratio

1. 1 : 3
2. 3 : 7
3. 10 : 7
4. 4 : 9
5. 1 : 2 : 4
6. 17 : 4 : 13
7. 24 : 27 : 32
8. 14 : 7 : 4
9. 8 : 2 : 5
10. 7 : 12 : 3
11. 2 : 3 : 5
12. 24 : 15 : 10
13. 9 : 4 : 22
14. (a) 3 : 2
    (b) 2 : 5
    (c) 5 : 3
15. (a) 1 : 36
    (b) 9 : 4
    (c) 36 : 1 : 16
16. (a) 1 : 50
    (b) 2 : 9
    (c) 11 : 450
    (d) hire more teachers

Proportion

1. 20
2. 12
3. 40
4. 3
5. 15
6. 5
7. 64
8. 4
9. 45
10. 56
11. 4
12. 4

13. 24 girls

14. 10 books

15. 2 desktop

16. 150 boys

17. (a) 1 : 3

    (b) 40 grams

    (c) 450 grams

18. (a) 25 white cars

    (b) 2 : 2 : 1

Similar Shapes

1. $x = 14, y = 6$

2. $x = 10, y = 9$

3. $x = 9, y = 2.5$

4. $x = 25, y = 32$

5. 160 cm

6. 5 m

7. 189 cm

8. 9 pixels

9. 62.5 cm

10. 37.5 m

11. (a) 24

   (b) $\frac{1}{24}$

   (c) 1.5 cm

12. $\frac{1}{200}$

Algebra

Using Letters for Unknown Values

1. $x + 3$

2. $p - 9$

3. $6h$

4. $\frac{y}{3}$

5. $\frac{5+s}{4}$

6. $2k - 17$

7. $\frac{s}{8} - 6$

8. $12b - 4$

9. $\frac{5f}{3}$

10. $\frac{14}{m} + 6$

11. $40 + b$

12. $11c$

13. $163 - d$

14. $\frac{p}{5}$

15. $80 - 15r$

16. $2m + 5$

17. $884 - \frac{y}{6}$

18. $34t - 126$

Simple Equations

1. 6

2. 14

3. 3

4. 18

5. 5

6. 58

7. 9

8. 49

9. 4

10. 50

11. 63

12. 4

13. $b + 14 = 35, 11$

14. $p - 5 = 4, 9$

15. $15n = 270, 18$

16. $\frac{c}{16} = 5, 80$

17. $\frac{g}{3} - 8 = 2, 30$

18. $4t + 15 = 27, 3$

19. $2e - 13 = 9, 11$

20. $\frac{d}{6} = 5, 30$

Formulas

1. $A = 25$, $n = 1$

   $A = 21, n = 5$

   $A = 19, n = 7$

   (or any other reasonable answers)

2. $R = 5, d = 1$

   $R = 10, d = 2$

   $R = 15, d = 3$

   (or any other reasonable answers)

3. (a) 10 (b) 15

4. (a) 46 (b) 8

5. (a) 16 (b) 54

6. (a) 28 (b) 11

7. (a) 2 (b) $\frac{2}{3}$

8. (a) 10 (b) 21

9. (a) $T = I + 4$ (b) 40 (c) 8

10. (a) $C = 8b$ (b) 72 (c) 168

11. (a) $T = \frac{S}{20}$ (b) 14 (c) 37

12. (a) $r = 26P$ (b) 234 (c) 598

13. (a) $C = 50 + 4g$ (b) 114 (c) 194

14. (a) $S = 12r + h$ (b) 63 (c) 102

15. (a) $S = 8d + 14n$ (b) 298 (c) 616

Number Sequences

1. 17

2. $-6, \ldots$

3. 92

4. 20

5. $6\frac{1}{2}$

6. $-\frac{1}{2}$

7. 3.4

8. 1.1

9. Yes

10. No

11. Yes

12. Yes

13. No

14. Yes

15. 9, 13

16. 19, 27, 43

17. 8

18. $\frac{3}{5}$, 1

19. 0, 10, 15

20. $-1\frac{1}{10}, -2\frac{1}{10}$

21. 4th row: 21 singers

    5th row: 26 singers

22. 1650 meters

23. (a) +3

    (b) 22 marbles

24. (a) 22 bricks

    (b) 114 bricks

25. (a) 13.8 degrees

    Celsius

    (b) after 8 minutes

26. (a) $1\frac{1}{4}$ pound

    (b) $6\frac{3}{4}$ pounds

Measures

Time

1. 351
2. 222
3. 56
4. 26,700
5. 29 h 18 min
6. 1 h 43 min 6 sec
7. 26 h 12 min 45 sec
8. 2 h 47 min 3 sec
9. (a) 480 min (b) $9\frac{1}{3}$ days
10. (a) 253 min (b) 3 h 34 min

11. 38 min 20 sec
12. 27 min 12 sec
13. 1 h 49 min 26 sec
14. 3 h 24 min = 204 min
    204 ÷ 6 = 34 min
15. 8 h 10 min
16. 2 h 15 min
17. 7:45 p.m.
18. 13:25

19. 11:50 + 45 min + 4 h 35 min = 11:50 + 5 h 20 min = 5:10 p.m.
20. Original scheduled time for departure is 22:40 + 20 minutes = 23:00 Original scheduled time for arrival is 10:45 – 50 minutes = 9:55 Scheduled flight duration from 23:00 to 9:55 = 1 hour + 9 hour 55 minutes = 10 hours 55 minutes

Weight

1. 4.5 kg
2. 0. 361kg.
3. 5000 g
4. 1700 g
5. 82 g
6. 6.55 kg / 6 kg 550 g
7. 1.65 kg / 1 kg 650 g

8. 3.33 kg / 3 kg 330 g
9. 0.457 kg or 457 g
10. Cake flour
11. The puppy
12. 3.25 kg
13. 1.38 kg
14. 5 batches

15. 45.46 kg
16. 270 g
17. 1.92 kg
18. 33 g
19. Yes
20. No

Volume

1. 0.56 L
2. 3.58 L
3. 1640 mL
4. 80 mL
5. 1.94 L
6. 1.395 L
7. 7.488 L

8. 570 mL
9. 1.065 L
10. 1.16 L
11. 4.2 L
12. 12 glasses
13. 4.425 L
14. 1.441 L

15. 700 mL
16. 105.75 L
17. 52 minutes
18. A carton of milk
19. The bigger bottle
20. No

Length

1. 215 mm
2. 760 mm
3. 37.8 cm
4. 7800 cm
5. 1050 m
6. 0.95 m
7. 1.469 km
8. 0.02591 km
9. 6.427 km

10. 42.2 cm
11. 2.457 km
12. 4.6 mm
13. Book shelf
14. Brian biked more
15. The front door
16. 4.18 m
17. 4.5 m
18. 62.5 cm

19. 3.48 m
20. 84 cm
21. 5.4 m = 540 cm

   45 mm = 4.5 cm

   540 ÷ 4.5 = 120

   min = 2 hours
22. 3.2 km
23. 4.94 km

Geometry

Angles

1. ∠JKL 180° straight angle
2. ∠XYZ 97° obtuse angle
3. ∠PQR 90° right angle
4. ∠CAB 145° obtuse angle
5. ∠PQR 42° acute angle
6. ∠WVX 246° reflex angle
7. Right angle
8. Reflex angle
9. Acute angle
10. Obtuse angle

11. 79°
12. 125°
13. 30°
14. 47°
15. 51°
16. $x = 102°, y = 33°$

17. 30°
18. (a) 60°
   (b) At half past, the hour hand travels to the middle of 10 and 11. So the angle between the hour hand and minute hand is 225°.

Circles

1. 3 cm
2. 10 m
3. 0.5 km
4. 15.75 mm
5. 8 m
6. 52 km
7. 6 mm
8. 4.36 cm

Triangles

1. Right angled triangle/Scalene triangle
2. Acute triangle/Equilateral triangle
3. Obtuse triangle/Scalene triangle
4. Acute triangle/Isosceles triangle
5. Acute triangle
6. Acute triangle/Isosceles triangle
7. Perimeter = 30 cm, Area = 30 cm^2
8. Perimeter = 90 cm, Area = 180 cm^2
9. Perimeter = 18 cm, Area = 15.6 cm^2
10. Perimeter = 32 cm, Area = 48 cm^2
11. Perimeter = 24 cm, Area = 17.5 cm^2
12. Perimeter = 76 cm, Area = 263.5 cm^2

13. 18°

14. 64°

15. 56°

16. 71°

17. 54°

18. 34°

19. 44°

20. 27 cm

21. $168

22. Yes

23. 24

24. 68 cm

Squares and Rectangles

1. Perimeter = 48 cm,
   Area = 144 cm^2

2. Perimeter = 28 cm,
   Area = 49 cm^2

3. Perimeter = 9.6 cm,
   Area = 5.76 cm^2

4. Perimeter = 52 cm,
   Area = 144 cm^2

5. Perimeter = 82 cm,
   Area = 330 cm^2

6. Perimeter = 48 cm,
   Area = 95 cm^2

7. 15

8. 21

9. 9

10. 8

11. 12

12. 33

13. 31

14. 5

15. 14

16. $809.6

17. 254 cm^2

18. 136 cm

19. 576 m^2

20. (a) 1058 cm^2

    (b) 184 cm

Other Quadrilaterals

1. Rhombus

2. Parallelogram

3. Trapezium

4. Trapezium

5. Kite

6. Quadrilateral

7. 240.5 cm^2

8. 620 cm^2

9. 760 cm^2

10. 549 cm^2

11. 61°

12. x = 108°, y = 72°

13. 59°

14. 13°

15. Trapezium

16. (a) Kite (b) 120°

3D Shape

1. 729 cm^3

2. 735 cm^3

3. 520 cm^3

4. 540 m^3

5. 1320 m^3

6. 1170 m^3

7. 3 cm

8. 2 cm

9. 9 cm

10. 7 m

11. 4 m

12. 2 m

13. 18 m^3 15. 320

14. 416 cm^3 16. 1728

Coordinates

1. X (5, 1), Y (-4, -3), Z (2, -5)   6. (1, 7), (-4, -5)

2. D   7. (3, -1), (-3, 9)

3. C   8. (-4, 3), (-7, 9)

4. B   9. C

5. A   10. A

Statistics

Data Organization

1. (a)

Number of books read	Frequency
0	3
1	4
2	3
3	5
4	3
5	2

(b) 20

(c) 3

2. (a)

Height (cm)	Frequency
101 – 110	4
111 – 120	8
121 – 130	3
131 – 140	4
141 – 150	6

(b) 25

(c) 111 – 120 cm

3. (a) 85 (b) 47 (c) 14

4. (a) 22 (b) April

5. (a) 141 (b) 45 (c) 51 (d) 6

Pictograms, Bar Charts and Line Graphs

1. (a) Kathy (b) 15 (c) 5

2. (a) 30 (b) B (c) 2

3. (a) 5 (b) Ryan (c) Dan and Henry

4.

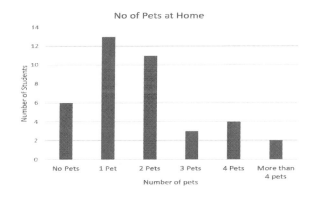

5. (a) 2003 and 2004

    (b) 2006

    (c) 2000 and 2001

    (d) The forest coverage has been decreasing.

6. (a) Wednesday

    (b)Sunday

    (c)Wednesday

7.

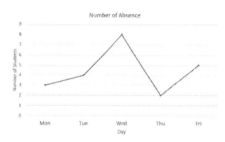

Pie Charts

1. (a) School   4.

    (b) Video game

    (c) 6 hours

2. (a) $350

    (b) Commission

3. (a) 90

    (b) 15

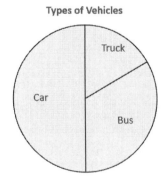

Venn Diagram

1. (a) Chocolate   2. (a) 5   (b) 4

    (b) 2   (b) 12   (c) 11

    (c) 4   (c) 25   (d) 6

    (d) 2   3. (a) 5   4. (a) 42

(b) 13   (c) Tablets

5.

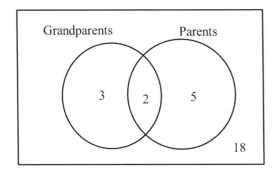

6.

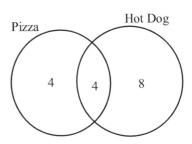

Mean

1. Mean = 7

   Median = 7

   Mode = 9

2. Mean = 30

   Median = 24

   Mode = 24

3. Mean = 50.75

   Median = 46

   Mode = 32

4. Mean = 43.875

   Median = 42

   Mode = 16, 45

5. Mean = 32.3

   Median = 31.5

   Mode = 22

6. Mean = 104.8

   Median = 100

   Mode = 72, 102

7. 3

8. 15

9. 7

10. 2.2

11. (a) smaller

    (b) unchanged

    (c) greater

12. (a) smaller

    (b) greater

    (c) greater

13. A

14. D

15. 9.25

16. (a) Ms. Ashley's class :129.3 cm

      Ms. Jenny's class: 125.4 cm

   (b) Ms. Ashley's class is generally taller.

17. (a) First phase:14.25 seconds

      Ms. Jenny's class: 12.65 seconds

   (b) The athlete improved his result in the second phase.

18. (a) 17 mm

(b) Yes, as the average rainfall in March is higher than the average rainfall in April.

(c) Yes, as mean/average is just a way to find the center where the data is distributed, and it is likely that some data is larger or smaller than the mean.

Probability

Introduction of Probability

1. $\frac{5}{14}$

2. $\frac{1}{6}$

3. Red

4. The total number of balls in the bag is 10. Therefore, the probability of picking a blue ball is $\frac{7}{10}$.

5. The total number of cups is 14. Therefore, the probability of picking a cup of coffee = $\frac{6}{14} = \frac{3}{7}$

6. (a) $\frac{2}{12} = \frac{1}{6}$

   (b) $\frac{3}{12} = \frac{1}{4}$

   (c) The probability of picking square is $\frac{1}{12}$. The probability of picking circle is $\frac{6}{12} = \frac{1}{2}$. Therefore, circle is mostly likely to be picked.

7. The total outcomes of two standard dices are 36. There are 6 outcomes that have the same number: (1, 1), (2, 2), (3, 3), (4, 4), (5, 5) and (6, 6). Therefore, the probability of rolling the same number with two standard dice = $\frac{6}{36} = \frac{1}{6}$.

8. (a) Out of 52 cards, there are 13 cards of diamond. Probability of picking a card of diamond = $\frac{13}{52} = \frac{1}{4}$

   (b) Out of 52 cards, there are 4 Kings. Probability of picking a King = $\frac{4}{52} = \frac{1}{13}$

   (c) Out of 52 cards, there are 26 red cards. Probability of picking a red card = $\frac{26}{52} = \frac{1}{2}$

(d) Out of 52 cards, there are 4 Queens. Probability of picking a Queen $= \frac{4}{52}$

Out of 52 cards, there are 13 cards of clubs. Probability of picking a clubs $= \frac{13}{52}$

Therefore, it is more likely to pick a card of clubs

BONUS MATH TEST

The content of this book has helped hundreds of students ace the ISEE/SSAT Lower Math. We are eager to hear how this book has helped you.

You can provide us with your feedback at;
expressllamz@gmail.com

As a thank you for providing feedback, we would like to provide you with a full Length Math test similar to the one at the beginning of the book.

This will enable you to measure your improvement and identify any weak areas to focus on.

Also, kindly report any errata/inaccuracies via the email above.

V0.6

Made in the USA
Columbia, SC
15 January 2020

86811890R00122